BREAKOUT

'I warmly commend Breakout to any church leaders who long to see the Holy Spirit releasing missional energy and imagination both among and through their people. The Mid-Sized Community approach (known in some places as Missional Clusters) is, in my view, one of the most strategic developments we have seen in the UK since the emergence of Alpha. I have already seen it being used effectively in two of our larger churches in the diocese of Canterbury, thanks to some excellent input from St Andrew's Chorleywood. But most important of all it is relevant to churches which are quite unlike St Andrew's – much smaller churches, with no plans to reorder their building. The core vision of enabling lay people to identify and own vision for a focused piece of mission, helping to gather others around them, and releasing and resourcing them to share the gospel in word and deed, can be followed almost anywhere, in any size of church. It releases the people of God for their God-given mission.'

Rt Revd Graham Cray, Bishop of Maidstone

'I think the tendency that we have, as Spirit-filled believers, is to get stuck in the "Bless me" culture: "If only I could get blessed one more time." This culture tends to keep the army in the barracks, and of course if the army is in the barracks the enemy has got the rest of the world. That St Andrew's is moving out of the barracks terrifies the enemy and his host, and signals an enormously important moment, a milestone, in English Christianity. What I have seen at St Andrew's is something that is not only important for St Andrew's but a model for other churches.'

Mike Breen, 3 Dimension Ministries and Senior Guardian of The Order of Mission

'I have found all that is happening in terms of mission-shaped communities at St Andrew's a fascinating and inspiring story. Mark and Andrew are honest about mindset changes, mistakes and wrong turnings, as well as the many good things which are emerging. St Andrew's has pioneered so many things over the last generation and is clearly at the forefront of another very significant development.'

Revd Dr Steven Croft, Archbishops' Missioner and Team Leader of Fresh Expressions

'Breakout *is a brilliant story of one church's journey into cultural significance. While many talk about the need for change in how we "do church", Mark Stibbe and Andrew Williams have actually caught the heart of God for their context and changed accordingly. While the reader may not copy the model exactly, it will be hard to read of this transition and not experience a shift in perspective along with a new-found hunger. It is a compelling and infectious story.'*

Bill Johnson, Senior Pastor, Bethel Church, Redding, CA, USA and author of *When Heaven Invades Earth* and *Face to Face with God*

'Breakout *is on the cutting edge of a new tidal wave of church life. One of the most difficult transitions a church can make is one that breaks long-held traditions. Whether it is the shift from consumerism to evangelism as Andrew calls it, from a cruise ship to a life boat as Mark describes it or from entertainment church to interactive church as I call it, Mark Stibbe and Andrew Williams have mapped the course that will equip a host of new leaders in the Body of Christ.'*

John Paul Jackson, Founder and Chairman, Streams Ministries

BREAKOUT

One Church's Amazing Story of Growth
Through Mission-Shaped Communities

**Mark Stibbe and
Andrew Williams**

Authentic

MILTON KEYNES • COLORADO SPRINGS • HYDERABAD

This book is dedicated to
all the unsung heroes of St Andrew's Church
Chorleywood who have embraced the call to
become a lifeboat church and worked tirelessly to
rescue the lost

Ecclesia reformata semper reformanda est

Contents

Foreword   xi
Mike Breen
Introduction   xiii
Mark Stibbe

1. The Winter is Over!   1
   Mark Stibbe
2. Coming in Off the Field   27
   Andrew Williams
3. Unlocking the Gold Reserve   44
   Andrew Williams
4. Finding the Dynamite   62
   Mark Stibbe
5. Breaking Out of the Box   87
   Andrew Williams
6. The Genius of 'And'   106
   Mark Stibbe
7. Following the Cloud   125
   Andrew Williams
8. Keeping the Glue Strong   162
   Mark Stibbe
9. Rumours of Reformation   191
   Andrew Williams

10. No Limits, No Boundaries   219
     Mark Stibbe

     Conclusion   245
     Mark Stibbe

     Bibliography   250

FOREWORD

This wonderfully engaging book offers a unique contribution to the story of worldwide church growth in the early third millennium. It offers wise counsel, frank admissions of failure, and timely reminders of priorities in the face of opposition and challenges.

St Andrew's is a pioneering church that has often been on the vanguard of where the Holy Spirit is leading the Church. This book functions as a helpful handbook for those seeking to successfully traverse this new and complex cultural landscape, making the transition from consumer-driven Attractional Church to more missional, entrepreneurial models that are community focused, discipleship based and seek to develop a leadership culture that is typified by high accountability and low control.

As Rector of St Thomas's Church in Sheffield, I often felt like a lone voice in the wilderness when trying to share our practice of Mid-Sized missional Communities (MSCs) which we called 'clusters'. When St Andrew's took up this model of missionary outreach, it felt like the small flotilla of churches already applying this principle had been joined by a battleship. Of course, these 'men o' war' vessels are not only equipped by God to do necessary spiritual warfare, but are also supplied with every gift needed to rescue those who are lost in the turbulent waters of our world.

xii   Breakout

The European Church Planting Network (ECPN) has
brought together key church planters from right across
the continent. As this work advances throughout Europe
and the rest of the world, we are seeing hundreds of
churches planted using the MSC model and thousands of
people coming to Christ. St Andrew's takes its rightful
place as part of this movement and has enriched the
learning community with its experience, honesty and
insights. The church in Chorleywood continues to be an
oasis of teaching, ministry and mission, and it is remarkable that the church has produced such creative and
diverse movements as New Wine and Soul Survivor.

Mark Stibbe is one of the world's great Bible teachers,
a deeply insightful prophet and a profound theologian.
It has been thrilling to read about the clarity of God's call
to lead St Andrew's and the great ways that God has
blessed this courageous leader and grace-filled church. I
have no doubt that St Andrew's will miss him greatly,
but his calling to bring the Father's love to the fatherless
is heartfelt, deep and irresistible.

Drew Williams is one of the best missional practition-
ers I have seen and it has been a privilege to get to know
him over the last few years. His practical and humble
style of teaching is deceptively profound – his wise and
gracious insights are impacting churches across Europe
and America.

My prayer is that God will use this profound story to
speak to you, helping you hear God's call upon your life,
and that you would be brave enough to step out, without fear, into his perfect plan for your life and local
Church. I wholeheartedly commend this book to you
and look forward with eager anticipation to the next
phase in the life of this wonderful Christian community.

Mike Breen

INTRODUCTION

As a child I loved my seaside holidays by the north Norfolk coast. I especially enjoyed the times exploring the lifeboat stations at Sheringham and Cromer. The stories of lifeboat rescues were well known around the coast. At times during the twentieth century, at least one lifeboat coxswain was more famous than Hollywood movie stars. These people were true heroes – ordinary people who did extraordinary things in order to save those at sea. I used to own a plastic replica lifeboat and play with it in the bath. I was inspired by the RNLI – the Royal National Lifeboat Institution.

I think it is fair to say that these childhood memories were formative in what has happened in St Andrew's Church Chorleywood over the last ten years or more. Before I became vicar, I spoke to a group of St Andrew's leaders about my vision for the future of the church. This was in November 1996. I brought RNLI posters of lifeboats and told them that the church was called to be a lifeboat station where everyone is working together to save those in peril on the sea of life.

In January 1997 I took up my post as Vicar of St Andrew's. Ten years later, in November 2006, I harked back to that earlier meeting as I addressed the whole church on our Commitment Sunday. I congratulated the people of St Andrew's as I pointed out that we were now indeed a lifeboat station with many mission-shaped communities meeting at the weekend, using extraordinary creativity to rescue those in peril on the sea of life. It had taken years of hard work but in the end we had seen the cruise liner church disbanded and witnessed instead many lifeboats launching. I remember thinking as I shared this, 'It's been worth it.'

Today, when I look at St Andrew's Church I see an inspiring picture. We have 440 people meeting at the centre every Sunday, dedicated to supporting and resourcing our rescue efforts. In addition we have 1,135 men, women and children meeting out in missional communities whose limit is fifty adult members and whose task is to serve the unchurched people they feel called to. We currently have thirty-two of these communities (with more in the pipeline), and they are led by unpaid leaders. They meet in coffee shops, school halls, community centres, Scout headquarters and other venues. They are highly mobile and they are focused on outreach. They are extremely effective and the source of much encouragement. They meet for two or three Sundays a month together, and on the fourth Sunday they come back to the church centre to be encouraged and re-envisioned. It is a remarkable thing that the Lord has done among us and we give him all the glory. This book is an attempt to tell the story – the Lord's story – in an honest way.

And honest is what it needs to be. If the truth be told, those of us in overall leadership have not always got it right. We have made some mistakes, and there is no getting away from that. Drew Williams and I are not going to hide these from you, because it is important we do not give the wrong impression about ourselves. We are imperfect people in the hands of a perfect Father.

At the same time, there are some lessons that can be learned from our failures and successes. We are not for one moment suggesting that every church needs to become exactly like St Andrew's. That would be foolish and proud. The Holy Spirit, after all, revels in diversity when it comes to mission. But we also know that there are some principles in what we have learned – often the hard way – that are of vital importance for churches in our post-Christian continent. In telling the story of what has happened at St Andrew's over the last decade or so, we encourage you to study the principles, not just the practices. There is simply no 'one-size-fits-all' approach to winning the west for Christ.

To put it briefly, our story is that of a painful journey from being a cruise ship church to being a lifeboat church. It could also be described as the story of a perilous passage from consumerism to evangelism. In my first five years at St Andrew's, I tried to reach the consumer culture with consumerist means. In doing so, I created a cruise ship. In my second five years, my Heavenly Father taught me that this was not the way to win people to Jesus, and he turned us inside out, creating a lifeboat church in which everything we do has a 'go to them' rather than a 'come to us' dynamic.

Leonard Ravenhill once said this:

> The Church used to be a LIFEBOAT . . . now she is a CRUISE SHIP. We're not marching to Zion, we're sailing there with ease . . . In the Apostolic church it says they were all amazed and now in all our churches everybody wants to be amused. The Church began in the upper room despised, in the upper room with a bunch of men agonizing, and it's ended up in the supper room with a bunch of women organizing. We mistake rattle for revival and commotion for creation and action for unction.

That is a truly challenging statement. I believe with all
my heart that we are called in the UK to develop lifeboat
churches, not pleasure boat churches. At St Andrew's we
have sought to do this. Although it has taken longer
than anticipated to change the culture, the vast majority
of our people have embraced this paradigm shift and
faithfully served the vision as Partners in Rescue. Drew
and I know that we couldn't have done this without the
partnership of well over a thousand workers. Like the
RNLI, we have few paid people and vast numbers of
volunteers. No rescues would happen without them,
which is why we have dedicated this book to the unsung
heroes of St Andrew's.

The year 2008 (when this book was published)
marked the one hundredth anniversary of St Andrew's
Church Chorleywood. St Andrew's was originally planted out from Christ Church Chorleywood, which today is
a vibrant church under the leadership of Revd Gavin
Collins. Originally, St Andrew's did not meet in a conse-
crated church building. In fact, that was not to happen
until 1966. It met instead in a hall which is now our
church hall. At that time it was called 'the St Andrew's
Mission Room'. The congregation was small, about the
size of one of our mid-sized communities today. It was
not buildings-dependent; in fact, for a while the congregation met in the Sportsman Hotel in Chorleywood. It
was only at the end of November 1908 that this group of
pioneers took up residence in the building on Quickley
Lane that we now refer to as 'the Lower Hall'.

One hundred years on I can see how something of the
DNA from our genesis as a church is now visible in the
establishing of many mission-shaped communities
meeting in community halls, schools, cafés and shelters.
Our forefathers knew a thing or two about what we're
doing today. Although the last ten years have seen new

things, these are a continuation of some very important 'older things' too. It is important in telling this story to remember that those of us who are living in such favour today are the beneficiaries of the mission-shaped vision of the vicar and people of Christ Church Chorleywood and the original heroes of St Andrew's.

So thank you, Christ Church, thank you to all previous clergy and members of St Andrew's, thank you to the present pioneering congregation, and thank you Heavenly Father!

Revd Dr Mark Stibbe, January 2008

1

THE WINTER IS OVER!

Mark Stibbe

Our story begins in 1994.

At the time I was Vicar of St Mark's on the edge of Sheffield and I was meeting one afternoon with a group of Christian leaders. We were praying together for clear direction from the Holy Spirit for our churches and ministries. Deep in prayer, I suddenly had a vision of the most beautiful and regal of animals – a stag. All I could see was its head, turned towards me, with dark brown eyes that were filled with love. I had a great sense of being wooed, as if this animal was inviting me to go from where I was and to follow in his direction. I opened my eyes and rubbed them. Then I went back into prayer. Immediately the same scene presented itself. I opened my eyes and rubbed them again. Then I closed them, only to be confronted afresh by the same striking vision.

At this point I had a very strong sense that the Holy Spirit was speaking to me prophetically, so I waited on him for an interpretation of the vision. Straightaway I was given a Scripture reference, Song of Songs 2:8–13. I had never read this passage before, so I had no idea what I was about to find. I opened my Bible and the first words I encountered were

1

Listen! My lover!
Look! Here he comes,
leaping across the mountains,
bounding over the hills.
My lover is like a gazelle or a young stag.
Look! There he stands behind our wall,
gazing through the windows,
peering through the lattice.

I was astonished. What were the probabilities of finding a Bible passage that mentioned a stag? With eager-
ness I looked more closely at the passage, and I sensed
the Holy Spirit reminding me that the Song of Songs
can be read at two levels. At the literal level, it
describes the intense love between Solomon and the
Shulammite woman. At the spiritual level, it describes
the intimate relationship between Jesus, the
Bridegroom, and his bride, the church. As I read the
first few lines of the passage in Song of Songs 2:8–13, it
seemed to me that Jesus was standing outside the door,
inviting his church to come out of the house to where
he was.

This was reinforced for me as I read on:

My lover spoke and said to me,
'Arise, my darling,
my beautiful one, and come with me.
See! The winter is past;
the rains are over and gone.
Flowers appear on the earth;
the season of singing has come,
the cooing of doves
is heard in our land.
The fig tree forms its early fruit;
the blossoming vines spread their fragrance.

Arise, come, my darling;
my beautiful one, come with me.'

It did not take long for me to understand what the Holy Spirit was saying. I sensed Jesus saying to his bride, the church, 'The season of hibernation is over. It's time to come out of the house. Don't stay indoors. The season has changed. It's time to come outside and pick the flowers.'

Catch the fire

'Yes, but how?' I asked.

I had been appointed Vicar of St Mark's at the end of 1992 and had taken up my post in January 1993. We were seeing some life and growth in the church, but I couldn't see how these words applied to my ministry in St Mark's. All I did know was that I had been told that there was a change in the seasons on its way, a change in which the church in this nation would move 'out of the house' at the invitation of the Bridegroom, and start to see life in places where there had formerly been barrenness. As for how that might happen in St Mark's, I was far from sure.

Then a very curious thing happened. In 1995 I was invited to go and speak at St Andrew's Church in Chorleywood. I had of course heard of St Andrew's. Under Bishop David Pytches' inspiring leadership, many great things had happened in the 1980s and the early 1990s. John Wimber and his team visited St Andrew's at Pentecost 1981 and there was a great outpouring of the Holy Spirit, leading to significant growth. Churches had been planted, including Soul Survivor Watford (led by Mike Pilavachi). Matt Redman had

begun his high-impact worship-leading and song-writ-
ing ministry there. And New Wine summer camps –
attracting tens of thousands – had been born from the
church as well.

When David Pytches invited me to come and speak at
St Andrew's, deep down I felt very honoured. His invitation was to come and speak at a midweek evening at
one of his 'Catch the Fire' gatherings in the church.
These meetings were being held each week in response
to the great hunger for more of the presence of God that
had followed the outpouring of the Holy Spirit at the
Toronto Airport Fellowship (at that time a Vineyard
church) in January 1994. Hundreds were coming to these
'Catch the Fire' events at St Andrew's, desperate for
more of the Lord, and people were being saved, healed
and set free by the Father's love. I decided I would go
and speak on the vision of the stag and the call to come
out of the house and follow Jesus into the harvest fields.

Having said yes to the invitation, I drove from
Sheffield to Chorleywood. As I drove down the M1 and
onto the M25, I saw a signpost indicating that I was now
in Hertfordshire. There was a stag on the sign.

I left Junction 17 of the M25 at about 6 pm, and as I
drove up Long Lane into the village of Chorleywood I
was greeted by a pub on my left called The Stag. The
pub sign had a beautiful painting of a stag on it too, not
unlike the one I had seen in my vision. I turned right
opposite the pub, down a road called Stag Lane.
Everywhere I looked, it seemed there were signs with
stags.

An hour or so later, I was in the chapel of St Andrew's
Church, being prayed for by a team of people prior to
the 'Catch the Fire' meeting. A man I had not met before,
but whom I knew by reputation, arrived late. His name
was Barry Kissell. He had been away praying on a quiet

day. He introduced himself to me and the conversation went something like this:

    'What are you preaching on tonight – the stag?'

    'Yes,' I replied, astonished.

    'Song of Songs 2:8–13?'

    'Yes, exactly.'

    'The winter is over?'

    'Yes. How on earth did you know that?'

    'I have been away praying all day today and that is what the Lord told me you would be speaking about.'

I can be quite slow at times, but even I appreciated at that moment that I was in the presence of a very unusual and prophetic man and I was greatly encouraged – which is exactly the effect genuine prophecy should have. I was encouraged because I realised that the message I had for the evening was truly given by the Holy Spirit. And I was encouraged because I felt a sense of connection with St Andrew's as a place. I felt like I belonged, that somehow this place had an immense significance for me personally.

The call to St Andrew's

We had a wonderful evening, as I recall, and then, after experiencing great hospitality in the vicarage from David and Mary Pytches, I drove back to Sheffield the next morning. Looking back today, I can see that that evening was a critical moment in my life. I had been prepared to give the rest of my life to the wonderful people of St Mark's and had told the Lord that I was ready to do that, if that was what he wanted. As soon as I surrendered all to him, things began to change. I remember sitting in the bath in March 1996, thinking about celebrating Easter at St Mark's, and the Holy Spirit clearly spoke to me and said, 'You won't be here next Easter.' Friends of mine told me that David Pytches was leaving St Andrew's Chorleywood and encouraged me to go and have a look at the church. Others prophesied over me that I was going to be David's successor. It seemed as if transition was imminent.

Perhaps the most remarkable of many clear instances of guidance occurred over a weekend in April 1996. I decided to go and have a look at St Andrew's the Sunday after Easter day. This is known as Low Sunday by many Anglicans. It is also a Sunday that many vicars take off, after the very demanding schedule up to and including Easter. I was taking a few days off work myself, and chose to drive to Chorleywood and stay with my good friends Rob and Anna Richards, to discuss the vicar's role at St Andrew's, and go to the Sunday morning services.

Driving down the M1, I was thinking about my time in Sheffield. I had been there over three years and was wondering what it was all about. I was asking my Father, 'What has been your purpose in this time-frame? I haven't seen the revival that I've longed and prayed for. In many ways it has been a really tough time, with many hardships and very few encouragements. What's it all about?' As I continued in this vein I remember distinctly sensing that I should look at 1 Kings 17. I pulled over and read in my Bible the story of Elijah spending three and a half years in a place called Kerith (a dried-up stream), living off the morsels that ravens brought to him. As I read that, I felt as if the lights came on in my heart. I began to see my three years or so at St Mark's as 'Elijah years' – wilderness years of refining and character formation, in preparation for a much bigger challenge to come, a challenge that would feel like Carmel. Weeping, I set off again on the M1 towards

Chorleywood. Almost immediately, the grey and overcast sky that had been with me for several hours on my journey turned to bright sunshine. Hope filled my soul for the first time in a long while.

That weekend at St Andrew's transformed my life. Several things stand out for me, both of which occurred on the Sunday morning in the 9.15 am service.

First of all, a man called Peter Maskrey was preaching. He didn't know me and I didn't know him. I was sitting towards the back of the church, next to Rob and Anna Richards. His message that morning was all about the next leader of St Andrew's Chorleywood. I recall it very vividly. It was based around Joshua 1:1–9 and was an inspiring description of the kind of leader St Andrew's needed next. Towards the end of his message he reached out his arm, pointed towards me at the back of the church, and uttered the following words: 'And who knows – maybe the next leader might be out there right now, thinking, "Am I the one God is calling to St Andrew's?"' It was astonishing. I could have fallen off the pew.

The second thing was equally remarkable. A lady called Joan was sitting behind me, who did not know me. In the middle of the service, she heard the Holy Spirit saying to her, 'The man sitting in front of you is called Mark and he is the next Vicar of St Andrew's.' After the service she went up to Barry Kissell, who had been leading the meeting (David Pytches was away on holiday). Joan told Barry what she had heard, and later the conversation was reported to me.

April 1996 was accordingly a momentous month for me personally. A few days later I found myself speaking at a conference organised by Anglican Renewal Ministries (ARM). The other main speaker was Marc Dupont from Toronto. We had never met before.

Without knowing anything of my situation, he turned to me at one point in the conference and said, 'The Lord says to you that you are like Elijah. You have been three and a half years in a dried-up stream, living off the morsels of encouragement that the ravens have been bringing. But this year, 1996, is the year of coming out of the wilderness. The Lord says he is about to put you in a new place where you will no longer be isolated but you will have strong men and women standing alongside you. So get ready!'

By the time I returned to Sheffield I was beginning to believe that we were about to move as a family. There was much to discuss with my wife Alie.

New beginnings

Alie and I found ourselves at Soul Survivor Warehouse in Watford. We were there for a day of interviews for the post of vicar at St Andrew's Church. Three other men were present for the same purpose, all three of them, humanly speaking, older, wiser and more equipped than me to be the next vicar.

It was a strange day. My flesh kept saying, 'You haven't got a chance. Look at these other men. They are way ahead of you.' In my spirit, I felt entirely different. I sensed the peace of the Lord that passes all understanding. I felt very serene and at rest within. I kept remembering one of my favourite sayings: 'The Lord doesn't call the equipped. He equips the called.'

That evening – on Friday 13 September 1996 – I received a phone call inviting me to consider becoming the next Vicar of St Andrew's Chorleywood. Without delay I said an immediate yes and put the phone down. Now I had the work of telling the staff and people of St

Mark's I was leaving, and my family had to prepare for a move to the south of England. We had about four months (September to December) to get ready to move house.

During that time I had to honour an existing appointment and spend three weeks in a seminary in Sweden, teaching on the work of the Cross and the Spirit. These lectures were later to be turned into a book called *Fire and Blood*. Perhaps the most memorable moment during those weeks away was when Alie phoned me to say she had had the most powerful vision she had ever received. I will leave it to Alie to describe exactly what happened, but it greatly challenged and influenced us both:

> I had retired upstairs to our bedroom with Sam, who was just four months old. I do not know how long I had been asleep, but I remember coming round from the unconsciousness of sleep to the feeling of being lifted up from the bed. I remember thinking that I was leaving my baby behind and wondering if he would be all right, but the feeling was only momentary as I felt completely enveloped by a sense of complete assurance. This was not an out-of-the-body experience, because I could not see my body on the bed, just a sense that Sam was still down there.
>
> The feeling of being lifted up continued until my vision was filled with a golden vista. The best I can compare it to is looking out of an aeroplane window across the clouds as the sun rises, but this is a totally inadequate picture of what I actually saw. The atmosphere was so thick that it was almost tangible, but there was nothing to touch; the light was intensely golden bright, yet soft and enveloping; the silence was complete, yet the air vibrated with 'noise' that was beyond human hearing but which I could sense all around me.

I suppose I should have been scared, but all I can remember was feeling an incredible sense of peace beyond description and wishing that I could stay in this place for ever. The second my mind uttered this desire, I found myself falling back down through the 'clouds'. The descent was fast, yet slow and controlled – I was not frightened, but just wondered what was coming next.

As I came out of the clouds I saw a large white structure. It was like a large marquee of the type that tent mission meetings used to be held in. As I got closer I could see people streaming out of the tent, perhaps six abreast, fanning out somewhat as they moved away from it. I came to earth on some grass to the left of the entrance; my back was to all the people who were coming out of the tent. I knew they were there, but in a sense I was on my own. As I looked ahead of me, a horizontal column of grey and silver cloud came around from the back of the tent. The cloud was very distinct in outline and direction. I remember being rooted to the spot and feeling an incredible sense of holy fear.

At this point I suddenly found myself wide awake in my bed. Absolutely wide awake: none of the pounding heart and racing pulse that usually accompanies being woken from a bad dream – I was completely awake, no bleary eyes, no racing pulse, no disorientation.

It was very strange. The light was shining in from the landing, as I always leave it on when Mark is away. As I sat there, making a mental note that Sam was still there and breathing, I asked in my heart what it was that had happened to me. Immediately I heard the words in my mind: 'When the Spirit comes, he will convict the world of sin, righteousness and judgement.' I knew these were words of Jesus from the New

Testament, but they were not any that I had read within years of that moment. I decided that I should ring Mark in Sweden. I described to him what had happened and he told me (being a leading expert on John's Gospel) that the words that had come to my mind were from John 16:8–11. Mark seemed to think that what had happened to me was a vision of the coming revival, but beyond that we had no idea what it might mean.

Now, in 2008, we are a lot clearer about it all. The large tent I saw is a symbol of 'gathered church', in which people are expected to come to hear the gospel – the traditional tent meeting format. The fact that people were streaming out of the tent rather than into it seems significant in relation to the outward-focused nature of the mission-shaped church strategy we have at St Andrew's. People are going out to win others for Christ, and the power and glory of God's Holy Spirit – the silver-grey cloud that I saw – is going out with them and before them to convict the world of sin, righteousness and judgement in a way that we have not experienced for many years.

I know from my academic study of visionary experiences that our interpretation of what we or others see and experience is very subjective, yet I can see no other reason why I should have been given such an experience right before Mark was about to embark on a journey to turn around a church in such a radical way, other than to encourage him that he was going in the right direction.

I do hope that what I have described brings some authenticity and a sense of God's sanction to the events that have unfolded at St Andrew's over the last eleven years. It has been an exciting time and we look forward with anticipation to what the Lord will do in the next phase.

A PCC with a difference

That was in November 1996. When I returned from
Sweden I was asked to pop in to a PCC meeting at St
Andrew's Church. The PCC in an Anglican church is the
Parochial Church Council, a body of elected representa-
tives of the church who are supposed to work with the
vicar in implementing the mission of the church. This
group had asked me to come and share the vision that I
had for the coming years at St Andrew's. Even though
I wasn't due to begin my ministry until 18 January 1997,
I already had a very clear sense of what the Lord was
saying, so I agreed.

On a cold November evening I went to the St
Andrew's PCC meeting – again in the chapel – and I
asked each member to consider in small groups the following question: 'If St Andrew's were to be compared to
an ocean-going vessel, what would it be?' I gave a few
suggestions for them to choose from and then let them
get on with their discussions.

Twenty minutes later each group fed back their
views. Some felt that the church should be a hospital
ship, others a battleship, still others an oil tanker. After
all had shared I was asked what I felt. I said that I saw
St Andrew's as a lifeboat church – as a place where we
were called in the future to move into radical mission
mode, intentional about saving those in peril on the
sea of life. I told them that I thought the Lord's will
was to create many new lifeboats and to send us out in
evangelism, and that this would usher in the revival
we were all praying for. I shared that the Holy Spirit
was saying to the churches, 'The winter is over. It's
time to come out of the house.' I also mentioned Alie's
powerful vision of the Holy Spirit moving outside the
tent.

Before I left the meeting, I prayed for every member of the PCC with the laying-on of hands, asking the Lord to empower each one for mission. There were striking manifestations of the Spirit's power and I remember thinking, 'This is very different from the PCCs I have been used to over the last fifteen years of Anglican ministry!' I had been an ordained staff member in three churches and never witnessed such things before in a PCC. It gave me great hope for the future that a group like this was so open to the Holy Spirit.

Before I left I also had some RNLI posters put up in the church, just outside the chapel. These posters were pictures of lifeboat stations and lifeboats at sea. One of them showed a lifeboat going down a ramp into the sea on a rescue mission. The words on the poster read quite simply, 'It's Time to Launch.'

A few weeks later, my family and I moved to Chorleywood. We arrived on 7 January 1997. My wife had flu. It was snowing. And we had a six-month-old baby needing constant attention. We had also had to stay unexpectedly in a hotel overnight. It was an extremely posh hotel. The only problem was we were broke, and paying the bill threw us into financial difficulties. In addition, my beloved father Philip Stibbe was very seriously ill and we were deeply worried about his health. All in all, it was a challenging time.

Somehow we got through the next few days, surrounded by boxes, trying to make our home at St Andrew's vicarage. Then the news broke that Dad was dying and I had to leave Alie and the children and drive at speed to the Norfolk and Norwich hospital. It was 16 January – a rather dark day in our family's history. For one thing, we had acquired a black Labrador puppy called Holly, who had turned out to be completely untrainable. On the way to Norwich I had to return

Holly to the breeder, a tough enough task in itself. But then I went to be with my dad, who was no longer conscious. Overnight it became clear that he was dying and on the next day, Friday 17 January 1997, my brother Giles and I held his hand at his bedside. I read Psalm 23 over my father. Hearing is the last thing to go, and I am convinced I could feel the faintest of squeezes as I read, 'Surely goodness and mercy shall follow me all the days of my life, and I will dwell in the house of the Lord forever.'

That evening my father died and I drove back to Chorleywood. The next day I was inducted as the new Vicar of St Andrew's Church by the Bishop of St Albans, in the company of a crowd of witnesses. My mother and my brother were sitting on the front row, having pulled out the stops to be there. However, the roller-coaster experience of the previous ten days had taken its toll. Alie had to spend most of the service consoling a distraught six-month-old son, and I was struggling to hold back the tears after the great loss of my father.

Six days later I broke down at family tea. It was Friday, about 6 pm, and we were saying our prayers. I gave thanks for my dad and then could not hold myself together any longer. My wife and children gathered around me and laid hands on me in prayer. All I can remember is a voice inside saying, 'I'll be your Dad.' It was my Heavenly Father. Losing my earthly father, I found a new intimacy with my Heavenly Father.

No honeymoon period

It is often said that the first six months of a vicar's time in a new post are a honeymoon in which you can make major changes. In that time, there is supposedly such good will for the new person that the congregation cuts an unusual amount of slack. In the eyes of many they can do no wrong, and hope springs eternal.

That was not my experience at the start of my time at St Andrew's! The truth is, many people in the church found my emphasis on revival and evangelism very difficult. Part of the reason for this was that the previous season had mostly been about equipping God's people for the work of ministry in the power of the Spirit. David Pytches had done an amazing job of training people for this purpose. He had established a prayer ministry team which is quite simply the best I have seen anywhere in the world. He had started leaders' days and other conferences designed to empower God's people to be more effective in the gifts and the ministry of the Spirit. On his watch, New Wine summer conferences had begun (with a significant emphasis on equipping), as had retreats for leaders. It was a time of growth for the church. But the focus was really on the renewal of local churches, not on reaching those outside the church. As a result, my constant emphasis on the unchurched brought me into major conflict with some who had enjoyed the previous season.

Another reason had to do with my presentational abilities. To be perfectly honest, if I had my time all over again, I would do two things differently. First, I would have made some different choices as regards my staff team. I have learned since then that it is vital to have the right people on the bus before you clearly define where the bus is heading. To put it another way, if you want to see growth, first get your team in place. I will write more of this later because it is a vital but much neglected principle.

Secondly, I would have spoken much less about revival and much more on the Kingdom of God. The church was used to hearing teaching on the Kingdom.

This was what John Wimber had brought to St Andrew's in the early 1980s. This was the emphasis David Pytches had brought to the church as well. If I had my time over again I would speak of the need to see a fulfilment of John Wimber's dream for 'power evangelism' – proclaiming and demonstrating the Kingdom of God outside the church, on the streets, in our communities, in the workplace, and so on. Talking about the Kingdom would have been more effective than talking about revival. Truthfully, I didn't spend enough time listening to the story and tapping into the spirituality of St Andrew's Church – both of which were Kingdom-oriented – before launching into the new vision.

The first year was accordingly very difficult and no doubt much of it was of my own making. When I was appointed Vicar of St Andrew's I was only 35 years old. Even though I had been ordained nearly ten years and on staff at three Anglican churches (including the large and thriving community at St Thomas' Church Crookes, in Sheffield), I was still very young and relatively inexperienced, especially for the leadership of such a flagship church. By the end of my first year I was not in a good place. In fact, I was on a drip in High Wycombe hospital, suffering from blood poisoning. The church was not in a good place either. If we had started with about six to seven hundred members, we had certainly lost at least one hundred and possibly many more.

Who says leading a large church like St Andrew's is easy?

It takes eight years

The next few years were full of challenges. We tried everything to make the vision of the church happen. The call was very definitely out to the lost, and we tried a number of things to kick-start the momentum for mission. We first of all put on seeker services. Seeker services are services geared towards those who do not come to church, pioneered by Bill Hybels and his Willow Creek Community Church in Chicago. With the very able help of J.John, we put on many events done with great excellence. J.John preached his now famous Ten Commandments series for the first time at St Andrew's. John and I also pioneered movie sermon series – guest services in which we used contemporary films as illustrations for the Gospel. We did these for years and we did them as effectively as we could. But in the end we did not see the evangelistic growth we longed for. If I am really honest, we saw many Christians in our region coming to these guest services, but far too few unchurched people.

In addition to seeker services we ran Alpha courses twice a year. In my first five years we never had many unchurched guests at these courses, certainly not as many as I would have expected. There was one course where we saw more, when my good friend Revd Greg Downes was on staff. Greg was and is one of the most effective evangelists I have ever met. He and his wife Tamie essentially went out and invited many of the guests themselves. We had about sixty for the course they ran, and every single non-Christian made a commitment to Christ. This was an exceptional time.

To be frank, we tried just about everything. We tried to apply the principles of the cell church movement. Both Rob Richards and Jim Sutton tried in successive phases to woo our ailing small groups to adopt a more outward focus. But this too was unsuccessful in establishing an outward momentum in mission.

At the lowest point, I remember J.John inviting me to his house up the road in Chorleywood to meet a great man of God – an English-born Australian called Phil Baker. Phil is the senior pastor of Riverview Church, the largest church in Western Australia. He had taken this church over from his father and had completely transformed the focus from inward to outward looking. I asked him how long it had taken him to see the church embrace this transition fully. He refused to tell me until I practically forced it out of him. Eventually he said, 'I don't want to tell you because I don't want you to be discouraged. But if you must know, it took me eight years. That's about the length of time it takes to change the course of a large church.'

One other major insight came out of my conversation and friendship with Phil Baker. He spoke about the front door and the back door of every church. He said the front door is the way in for those who do not go to church. How does a church make a big and welcoming front door? The answer is to increase your evangelistic potency (EP) and your invitational ratio (IR). In other words, you have got to make your church services more welcoming for those who do not go to church. You have to increase the evangelistic potential of your main worship events. At the same time, you have to motivate your church members to go out and invite the unchurched to these events. You can have the greatest EP in the world, but if your IR is low then it is all to no avail. Creating a big and welcoming front door is dependent on increasing EP and IR together.

At the same time, the back door of every church needs to become smaller. In many churches the back door is bigger than the front door. So you have a few people coming in and a lot going out. The key is to close the back door. This is closed by dealing with two things. The first is your retention rate (RR). When new people come to your church, you have to retain them. In other words, you need to have a structure in place to make sure they are discipled in community and then stay in community. At the same time, you need to be aware of your attrition rate (AR). This is the natural attrition of church members who leave the church for reasons that you cannot control but which at the same time you have to be aware of. So, for example, some church members move house and others of course die.

Phil Baker's insights into church growth through evangelism were an eye-opener for me. What I saw straightaway was that we had increased our evangelistic potency as a church – through seeker services, Alpha etc – but these were not working effectively because our invitational ratio was so low. There was nothing inherently wrong with Alpha or with the seeker service concept, but the truth was we were not as a church inviting unchurched people. We all had lots of Christian friends but very few non-Christian friends.

Somehow, we all needed to get out more.

Finding your vehicle

In 2002–3, after several very difficult years, two things occurred in my life that had a massive effect on our future as a church.

The first was that I was invited to King's College London to an academic conference on Revival which took place in 2002. I was one of a number of theologians asked to address the conference on this subject, and these papers were published in the book *On Revival*, edited by Andrew Walker and Kristin Aune and published by Paternoster Press in 2003.

After giving my address, I went into one of the workshops and listened to a historian called Meic Pearse

speaking about the history of revival. His thesis was that
the traditional kind of revival – which he called 'meetings-driven' – was unlikely to happen in the future in
the UK. Our society is simply too post-Christian now.
He pointed to the phenomenal growth of Christianity in
China – a revival without church buildings, public meetings and great evangelists. He ended his session by saying that the UK was now so 'post-Christian' that the
China model of revival was the one most likely to happen in the west. As in China, a western-nation revival is
more likely to be a grass-roots movement of Christians
taking the Gospel out to the many people who have
absolutely no Christian memory, spending time gradually bringing them to faith. Pearse concluded that
'revivals in minimal-Christian-presence societies such as
ours tend to come from the hard work, prayer and witnessing of the many, rather than from the high-profile
pulpit declamations of the few'.

When I heard this it was as if the lights came on. I suddenly understood what I had been doing wrong. Going
back to 1994, the Holy Spirit had clearly spoken to me
before I arrived at St Andrew's – through the vision of
the stag and the passage from Song of Songs 2:8–13. At
that time he had told me that the seasons were changing
and that the church was not to stay indoors enjoying
Jesus all to itself but rather to come out of the house and
go and pick the flowers (i.e. bring people to life in
Christ). This was what Meic Pearse was saying at King's
College London, albeit in a less poetic way. How could I
have been so blind? When I saw the vision of the stag in
1994 I had received revelation, I had found the interpretation, but I had not engaged in the right application.
Ever since then I had been employing an inappropriate
model of reaching my community and region with the
Gospel. Instead of letting God's people go in mission, I

had called them to stay in the building and I had employed a meetings-driven model. I felt cross with myself for being so wrong.

The revival conference at King's College London was therefore a turning point for me. I suddenly saw that my theology of revival had been faulty. With the best intentions in the world, I had built a 'come to us' model of revival, while all the time Jesus had been inviting us to 'go to them'.

The following year, something equally significant occurred. I woke up one morning thinking about a friend of mine called Mike Breen. Mike and I had not spoken or communicated for about four years. Mike affectionately refers to this time as 'the hidden years'. In my heart I had secretly felt angry with him because he had let me know that the meetings-driven model of revival wasn't going to work. That had got me pretty mad and I had effectively gone into a four-year sulk.

Then one morning in the early part of 2003 I woke up feeling very sad about my lost friendship with Mike and I started to pray for reconciliation. At lunch that day, my friend John Coles (who heads up the New Wine movement) took me out for a pub lunch in Chorleywood. We chatted for a while and then I confessed to John how sorry I was that I had developed a bad attitude towards Mike. At this point John said, 'Well, let's pray about that now.' In the pub, we prayed for a miracle of restoration.

I said goodbye to John and went to the vicarage to tell my wife Alie about the amazing prayer for reconciliation with Mike Breen that John and I had just prayed. I then walked across the car park to my church office at St Andrew's. I was picking up my post and messages when the phone went and I heard my wife's voice at the other end. 'You'll never guess who's standing on our front doorstep.' 'Who?' I asked. 'Mike Breen,' she replied. 'Should I let him in?'

Alie did let Mike in, and I went over to the vicarage and confessed my unhealthy thoughts about him. He was extremely gracious and kind. We were quickly reconciled and went out for a meal together at a restaurant.

'What brought you to my front door today?' I asked.

'I was speaking at a conference half an hour away. I was just due to do the morning session and, while I was speaking, I asked the Holy Spirit what he wanted me to do with the rest of the day. Straightaway the thought came to me that Mark Stibbe is only half an hour away and I haven't seen him in years. So here I am.'

The Lord is sovereign! He really does reign. And he really is in control.

The conversation that followed helped to shape everything that has happened in the last four or five years at St Andrew's. As we ate, I asked Mike how I should lead St Andrew's out in mission. He took a napkin from the restaurant table and drew the following:

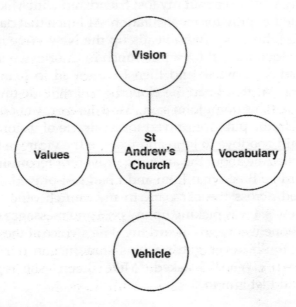

Mike shared that it is no good having a vision without a vehicle. In other words, if your vision is to go and reach the lost, it is imperative that you have the means to carry out that vision. In the same way, it is really important to be clear about your values and to have a vocabulary for describing these core values.

Mike went on to share about his church at St Thomas' Crookes – where I had been a curate during the previous vicar's time. He talked about his vision to take the Good News to the city of Sheffield. He spoke about what he called 'clusters', groups of about thirty to fifty people – missional communities led by entrepreneurial lay leaders both in Crookes and throughout the city. This was the primary vehicle for carrying out the vision. Then he spoke about the values and vocabulary that had been so essential for the implementation of this vision. At the time I spoke to him, St Thomas' Crookes had over two thousand members and was the largest Anglican church in the north of England.

Thirty minutes listening to Mike taught me more about dynamic, apostolic leadership than I had learnt in nearly thirty years as a Christian. It was utterly life-transforming and led to a total paradigm shift in my thinking. Alpha hadn't been wrong, nor had the seeker services. Both of these things can still work, but in our postmodern, post-Christian context we have to go out and establish long-term missional communities where non-Christians live and work if we want to have people to invite to meetings like these. That is what I had failed to see but which now, thanks to the two Mikes, I fully grasped. From this point on, nothing was going to be the same again. I had seen something from an entirely new perspective and it had transformed not only my thinking but my whole approach to spiritual leadership. Since that conversation with Mike Breen, I have been committed to a completely different model of mission. I have moved from a 'come to us' to a 'go to them' paradigm.

It all starts

The upshot of that meeting with Mike Breen was this. In the summer of 2003 I preached to the whole church over the course of a month about the four Vs. I clarified what our vision was – to bring the Father's love to those who are outside the church. After a long process of consultation with the staff and PCC, I clarified what our values were (more of that later) and sharpened up in the process on some of the vocabulary. The biggest challenge was 'vehicle'. We knew that the life of our church could not be determined by the Sunday meetings. These were quite impressive in terms of numbers, but many of the people were in fact visitors. I was acutely aware that the only other kind of community we had was small groups, and these were dying. So I announced that we were going to go into a massive season of change in relation to our small groups and that we were now actively looking for an associate vicar to come in and help us with that. We would be interviewing in September.

And so came what I regard as one of the most important days in my time as vicar at St Andrew's Church Chorleywood. In September 2003, two men arrived at St Andrew's with their wives. For the whole of that Saturday, members of my staff team, with the help of the Bishop of Hertford (Chris Foster), interviewed both. Both of them were outstanding candidates and, to be honest, we could have employed both. But only one was called.

After we had said goodbye to both couples, we dispersed to our own homes for a couple of hours of rest and prayer. Then we reconvened at the vicarage early in the evening to pool our thoughts about the two candidates for the Associate Vicar post. Both had performed impressively on the day. We had asked many questions about small group communities. We had asked them to complete an exercise about how they would address the issues we were faced with. Both were exceptional people.

There were about twelve people crammed into my sitting room at the vicarage. I went round asking every single one what they thought, and one by one they said, 'There's something about that guy Andrew Williams.' By the time everyone had had their say, I was absolutely convinced that Andrew Williams was the man to take on the challenge of helping us create suitable vehicles for our mission-shaped vision. He had shown unusual creativity in his answers and a great ability to think outside the box. He was not tied to what other churches were doing or to the latest fad in the church growth world. He was clearly an original thinker and a very prophetic person who heard the Lord. Most of all, it had become obvious during the course of the day that he was connected to us and indeed called.

So that night, as Drew and his wife Elena drove back through the darkness to Devon, I phoned them and invited Drew to take the role of Associate Vicar of St Andrew's Chorleywood, with a blank sheet of paper for doing whatever it would take to get all our people into smaller communities with an OUT focus.

Drew said yes. With that decision, God started to put the adventure back in our Christian venture.

It was truly a history-making moment, the beginning of a new Reformation for our church.

It was the moment when we got ready to obey the call of the Bridegroom:

> *'Arise, my darling,*
> *my beautiful one, and come with me.'*

2

COMING IN OFF THE FIELD

Andrew Williams

I was sure that the news would come by telephone, that there would be a call from someone somewhere saying, 'This is your next move.' I was very much enjoying my curacy. This was at another St Andrew's, but this one was tucked in the lee of Dartmoor in a west Devon village called Whitchurch. The church was growing in strength and number and the Father was very busy with us. I was the first curate they had received in five hundred years. I often wondered what the last one had done so wrong, but I was very grateful for this opportunity. St Andrew's Whitchurch was a fantastic start to my ordained ministry. So I had resolved not to look at the church papers and not to make enquiries but to wait for this prophetic telephone call. It's funny how despite all this inward resolve you still don't expect the call when it actually comes. It was my brother Paul ringing me on his cell phone from a supermarket in Watford: 'Drew, did you know they're looking for an associate vicar at St Andrew's Chorleywood?'

About a month before Paul made this telephone call we had spent some time in Chorleywood. Paul had returned from Brazil, where he had been working with

Happy Child, a Christian ministry working with street children in Belo Horizonte. The Lord had enabled Paul and his Brazilian wife Alessandra to return to the UK so that Paul could study at London School of Theology. Paul and Alessandra invited us up for half-term, and so my wife Elena and our two small girls, Katie and Isabel, squeezed into their one-bedroom apartment.

I was shattered. Paul took me for some long walks over Chorleywood common and gave me a rollicking about overworking and neglecting the family. They really looked after us, and at the end of each day we would eat too much Brazilian food and watch movies late into the night. The next day Elena and I would say that we could not possibly stay another night and they would persuade us that we should stay, and so the week went on. I think we had about four last meals together. And throughout our stay there was the strangest feeling that something significant was about to happen. I had said privately to Elena, 'God is going to do something.' I have a very clear memory of walking across Chorleywood common and saying to Elena that we could live here. So we kept on enjoying these last meals together until we came to Sunday, and then Paul said, 'Well, as long as you are here you might as well come to church with us on Sunday morning at St Andrew's.'

It was a family service and one of the children's pastors, Dave Hill, drove his moped up the aisle. The congregation was encouraged to inhale quickly three times to clear the church of exhaust fumes. I thought, 'I like this place.' At the end of the service Paul introduced me to Mark Stibbe. We got chatting and before I knew it, under some gracious interrogation, I had told Mark my testimony in about two minutes flat. Solicitor working in the city as a litigator who feels the call of God to return to rural roots in Devon, where he is soundly brought to faith and then baptised in the Holy Spirit in a disused railway shed. The same solicitor leaves law and gets ordained. Mark said, 'I am preaching tonight: can you and Paul give your testimony?' Elena was waiting in the car with the girls, expecting us to begin the journey back to Devon, when I said, 'Do you remember that I said the Lord was up to something?'

Under the bold title 'What is my destiny?' Mark was bravely using the movie *Minority Report* as a springboard to preach that night on free will and predestination. Paul and I were late. We were met at the church door by a very tall man with a very big smile, who ushered us into a side room where Mark was very relieved to see us. As Mark spoke about what he was going to say, I felt my concentration interrupted as the Holy Spirit spoke very clearly to me: 'You and Mark will work closely together and will become good friends.' I was shocked by the audacity of this thought. On the quiet, Mark was a bit of a theological hero of mine. In the first few hours of my being baptised in the Holy Spirit someone had pressed a copy of Mark's book *Times of Refreshing* into my hand and it had really spoken to me. Since then I had read just about everything he had ever written – which was a lot.

The Holy Spirit was insistent and this time his voice was overpowering: 'You and Mark will work closely together and will become good friends.' I was reeling. I could see Mark opening and closing his mouth but I had no idea what he was saying. I was led out into the auditorium and was desperately trying to work out by intuition and lip-reading what it was that Mark might have been trying to tell me about the evening. Part of me was thinking, 'For goodness' sake, will you just focus?' while another part was continuing in conversation with the Lord, and an extremely errant part of me was struck by how surprisingly thick the blue carpet pile was on the platform.

Another audacious moment was to follow. As I was answering Mark's questions on the platform (it really did have surprisingly thick blue carpet), I felt what I can only describe as an internal click: that moment when something that is perfectly fitted snaps into place. I looked out at the congregation and felt at home. There was a peculiar awareness of a heart connection with a church full of people that I had never met before. I got through Mark's interrogation and was beginning to breathe a sigh of relief when he bowled a final fast-ball question at me: 'So what is your destiny?' Internally my answer began, 'Well actually, I am waiting for a telephone call, so I can't be too specific, but you won't believe where I think I might be headed!' My external answer went along the lines of, 'I know that God has plans for me, plans to give me a hope and a future. I am not sure how all this will work out – the important thing is that my destiny is in Christ Jesus.' That seemed to satisfy Mark and the congregation. Paul said afterwards, 'What a horrible question – I am so glad he bowled that one at you!' We had to leave almost immediately: this time I really did have to drive the family back to Devon. Elena had been very clear about this. As we sneaked out, Belinda Patrick was leading the congregation in worship and the presence of God was there. I really did not want to leave. As we left the building, the Holy Spirit whispered, 'It's all right: you're coming back.'

Beginning with the letters 'C' and 'H'

Back at St Andrew's Devon, several months before these events, the weekly intercessory prayer group had gathered and they were very kindly praying for me. One member of the group spoke out an interesting picture that the Lord had shown her: a diary left open at June, with one of the pages turned down at the corner. She told the group that she believed the Lord was saying he had marked a new season out for me, beginning in June of this year. There was a general sense of agreement in the room, and then someone added, 'The Lord showed me that he will be sending Andrew somewhere that begins with the letters "C" and "H".' They then spent a few moments trying to think of as many places in Devon as they could that began with those two letters. Wisely, they did not talk to me about this.

And so the telephone call came. Paul broke the news from his mobile phone while he did the shopping and immediately I went off to find Elena to tell her the news. She said, 'I think this could be it.' A few emails passed. I stayed up until 4.00 am writing a CV and we waited. It all seemed so improbable and so unlikely and yet there was such a sense that the Lord was in it. I recall a very vivid dream at about this time. In the dream, my then boss and good friend Simon May welcomed me into his home and led me to the open back door, where sunshine was pouring in. In this dream he said, 'Andrew, St Andrew's Chorleywood is for you. The Lord has ordained it. All you have to do is to trust, have courage and be faithful.'

I was shortlisted, and on a sunny June weekend we drove up to Chorleywood for a day of interviews. My dad lent me his car and I recall that we listened to a Michael Ball CD all the way up the motorway because it was stuck in the car's CD player and we could not turn it off. I also remember feeling the benefit of so much prayer. We stopped at a motorway service station and I was so filled with the Holy Spirit (in response to the prayers of all our family and friends) that I asked to see the manager and complimented him on his fine latte and croissants. I can see the look in his eye even now: 'This guy needs to get out more!' Upon our arrival at Chorleywood, our hosts immediately put us at our ease. This was no small thing, because notwithstanding all the prayer, I don't think I had felt this nervous since I took my Law finals. I also remember that I bought a new suit for the interview. Mark turned up in shorts and with his dog, and has since ribbed me on how overdressed I was.

Anyway, the day went pretty well. I was asked to present a paper on what I would do with the small group structure. They had been very honest in telling me that the small group network was in need of a major overhaul, and I had pulled together a paper which set out some possible scenarios. My one original point, buried deep in my interview presentation, was that it might just be a good thing to draw small groups together into larger groups – that groups that were bigger than small groups but not as big as the congregation might be a creative environment to release mission and gifting.

Like most curates, I had led the youth group at St Andrew's Whitchurch. We had experimented with youth cells but had also drawn these cells together into clusters on alternate weeks. The different-sized groupings had brought a new set of operating dynamics to the way we worked. We had seen some growth in number and in faith and it seemed to me that there might be some potential here. That was as much as I had, hence the purchase of the new suit.

By about midday I had convinced myself that despite my fine attire and my one original thought, the other candidate was much better suited to the position and I would not be joining the church. Between interviews, Jim Sutton, an ordained member of the staff team and a wonderful man of God, invited Elena and me to have a cup of tea in his back garden. He and his wife Pat left us alone in the garden and I shared with Elena how I thought things were going. We prayed, and my wife and the Lord gave me a swift kick up the backside, and then Jim took us back to the church for the final interview. I recall Jim's very clear but unspoken encouragement as we returned. I don't quite know how he managed to impart the Father's love so powerfully without words but I felt my spirit lift within me. I met Mark and his wife Alie in the church car park. Mark said, 'If we were to offer you the job, how would we contact you later tonight?' That was all the encouragement I needed and the last interview was a blast. We said our farewells and I drove round to my brother's to tell him how it had all gone. I recall that he laid on a barbecue on the very small balcony of his flat.

As we drove home, the reality of what was about to happen began to sink in. I had discerned that St Andrew's was in for a season of significant and radical change and that there were some very great challenges ahead. There was silence in the car (we had managed to turn off Michael Ball) and I now felt sick at the prospect of what lay ahead. In the run-up to the interview I had been praying that the Lord would allow me to serve him at St Andrew's. Now the largeness of the task loomed and my feet were distinctly cold. Following the Lord's instruction, I had trusted, I had been faithful and courageous up to this point, but I was now under no illusion that what was coming was going to call for a lot more. Elena and I sat in silence in the car. I was taken up with my thoughts. And then the Lord said very gently but very firmly, 'Andrew, you have sought me on this appointment but now I am asking you: will you do this for me?' It was a simple question. My answer to Mark's fast-bowl question on the blue carpet came flooding into remembrance: 'I know that God has plans for me, plans to give me a hope and a future. I am not sure how all this will work out – the important thing is that my destiny is in Christ Jesus.' What else could I say but yes? So I said, 'Yes, Lord, if you are asking me to do this, then I will do it.' I recall silently shaping these words on my lips. This memory is so finely etched on my mind that even as I recall it now I can see the dashboard of my dad's car and the road ahead.

We were on the A303, just outside Andover (which in one of those little God touches was also the place of my birth), and as I completed my answer to the Lord's question Elena's phone rang. It was Mark: 'Andrew, the interview panel have met and prayed. We have unanimously voted. I would like to offer you the position of Associate Vicar at St Andrew's Chorleywood.'

So I said 'Yes,' for the second time that night.

Iron sharpens iron

Leaving St Andrew's in Devon was hard. Bizarrely enough, my mum and step-dad were in the congregation. When I came to faith, the first thing the Lord had asked me to do was to go and tell my brother. So I kept Paul up to date with all that the Lord was doing, and about six months later he gave in and quietly took himself off to Holy Trinity Brompton, where he was gloriously saved between the 5.00 pm and 7.00 pm services. Paul and I then turned our attention to our parents and within a few months my mum and step-dad attended an Alpha course at a thriving and Spirit-filled church called St Andrew's Whitchurch in Devon. They came to faith. That the Lord should have prepared this church for my curacy was a very neat bit of planning! After years of living at quite some distance, it was so good to have my parents close by. Our youngest daughter Isabel was born in the curate's house in Whitchurch, and these were very special and cherished years.

As we were getting ready to leave I had a call from a colleague, Graham Cotter, who was the vicar of a nearby parish church in Buckland. Barry Kissell, twenty-five years at St Andrew's Chorleywood, had led a faith-sharing mission to Buckland parish church many years before and great fruit had followed. Graham asked me if I could spare him a half-hour to say farewell and for us to pray together. As we prayed, Graham said that he had a picture of a vast ship that was in need of reordering. There were scattered chairs and containers strewn across the deck. He believed that the Lord was calling me to refashion this vessel, to draw the crew together in some new way. I was also given a verse, Proverbs 27:17: 'As iron sharpens iron, so one man sharpens another.'

At about this time I had another dream. I was walking with my boss Simon across beautiful sand dunes. It was evening time and we were chatting; I was asking him questions. We came to a gate which led to a large expanse of beach. Simon opened the gate for me and I passed through, continuing with our conversation. Only later did I realise that Simon was no longer by my side. I looked back and there he was on the sand dune, waving me off. I said, 'So this is it, Lord: it's just you and me now.'

So we said our sad farewells, packed up our belongings and followed the removal van from Devon to Hertfordshire. We arrived late in the evening of Elena's birthday and Mark and Alie showed us around our new home with their youngest son Sam. Things had moved so quickly that I had not even seen the house. The Lord had brought everything else together, so I was sure I could trust him with where we would live. He was faithful. It is a lovely family home with a crooked apple tree in the garden, where we immediately hung a swing for the girls.

The kitchen was so filled with gifts from church members that we could not see any counter space: baskets of fruit, flowers, biscuits, chocolates, wine. We were overwhelmed. Sam brought a book about large spiders for the girls to look at, and Mark commented that he had been tempted to eat some of the chocolates – but, he added, as the Lord is always watching us he had thought better of it. Alie, with characteristic candour, apologised for most of the curtains (which were indeed of their decade) and invited us for Sunday lunch. They prayed for us and then Paul and Alessandra (now expecting their first child) turned up with a birthday cake and candles for Elena. We sat in the empty sitting room, sang Happy Birthday and made a start on the biscuits.

Coming in off the field

A few weeks of unpacking, decorating and picture-hanging passed very quickly and then it was time to get on with the job. I had yet to be introduced to the church on a Sunday, so I had about a week to get my bearings with some anonymity. There were several visits from our new church family, who were incredibly kind in their welcome. I also recall answering the door one evening to a lady with a very pretty smile and a large bouquet of flowers. I was touched by this gesture and although I did not know it at the time, the Lord had just introduced me to my assistant, Judith Davies. Had I known this I would have had much more confidence for all that was to come. If Judith had appreciated that she was going to be stuck with me for the foreseeable future nobody would have blamed her for emigrating. Fortunately for me and for St Andrew's she stayed. Her contribution to the life of St Andrew's is incalculable, and on a personal note, that my wife and children saw anything of me over the coming years was largely down to Judith. We all love her very much and I will be forever in her debt.

Mark was teaching a series of midweek seminars on prophetic evangelism and asked me if I wanted to come along. I turned up in the church lounge and wondered if I should introduce myself, but thought better of it. The seminar was great, but at the end of the session a number of us were invited to come to the front; I found myself among that number. The rest of the class was then asked to seek the Lord and to prophesy over us. There was some prayer, some silence and then, tentatively at first, words were shared. It was astonishing to see this line-up of people reduced to tears as the Lord spoke words of encouragement over them with such striking accuracy. Then it was just me. I thought, 'How embarrassing. They don't know what to say to me.' And then one person looked up. 'This is a bit bold,' they began, 'but I think that you have a calling upon your life as a church leader.' Someone else said, 'Yes, I see that too. When I saw you I saw a shepherd with all the sheep pressed in around you, and you knew all their names.' Someone else said, 'Well, I see you as David, coming in off the fields – caked in mud – ready to serve the Lord.' 'You are definitely a pastor,' said another, 'and whatever the Lord is calling you to do, you are in it for the long haul.' Mark said, 'Drew, you had better tell them who you are!'

On the Saturday night before I was to be formally introduced to the church, I took a few things over to my new office. I also felt I needed some time with the Lord. I put down what I had been carrying and knelt before the cross. There was a refrain of an old worship song going round in my head but I could not call the words to mind. I prayed for a while and then looked down at the floor. On the ground were the objects that I had been carrying: a hammer and a set of keys. I knew what the Lord was saying. Here were some tools for a large job of reconstruction and release. Then one line of the worship song came to mind: 'Father God, you're there beside me . . .'

Sunday was a lot of fun. Some friends of ours had turned up to cheer us on and there was some confusion as to who I was married to, but we managed to sort that out. In the evening the staff laid hands on me in the service. I recall Jim Sutton's prayer very clearly: 'Andrew, the Lord has called you to begin a new work. I see a large map and you setting fires all over it.' And then he added with a wry smile, 'I believe the Lord is equipping you with bags of rich manure and a large box of matches!'

I concluded my first preach at St Andrew's with these words: 'Receiving the Father's love and giving it away: that is what you are known for and it has not been without sacrifice. I believe the Lord is lining us up to go out into the harvest fields, to give away his heart all over again. We are to have a new commissioning, a fresh anointing as the older brother. And this anointing will begin with a fresh revelation of his Father heart.' I had not the slightest idea how all this was going to work out, but I had a hunch that we would need a hammer, a large set of keys, some bags of well rotted manure and a box of matches. What on earth was the Lord about to do?

The gold reserve

And so the work began. In the beginning this was mostly about trying to remember everybody's name and visiting as many of the remaining small groups as I could find. I was handed a large red folder with details of all the small groups. On first sight, to read this folder was to ask why they had hired me. On closer examination it became clear that many of these small groups were subliminal groups, or at least they were operating on such a high spiritual level that their members never actually met. I would ask the question, 'Are you in a small group?' The reply would come: 'Oh yes, I belong to Mavis's small group. I have been a member of Mavis's small group for 140 years and we really love each other.' I would cautiously ask, 'And when did you last attend Mavis's small group?' To which would come the reply, 'Oh, that would have been about 1986.' Clearly Mavis's small group loved each other very much but could not stand the sight of each other. I think it would be fair to say that there was also some history of warm-hearted resistance to change. Rather tongue in cheek, one small group leader winked and said to me, 'We have successfully resisted all change for twenty-five years – what have you got to say to us?' Mark's PA at the time greeted me one morning with the encouragement, 'I really would not want your job.'

Whether I wanted the job or not, the facts were fast revealing themselves. We had a diminishing network of small groups that were disbanding faster than they were growing. Less than 12 per cent of the church were actively attending a small group. Not surprisingly in such a climate of decline, the small groups that were soldiering on were in survival mode and so increasingly there were signs of introspection. I recall one afternoon attempting to place a newcomer to the church in a small group and being told on several occasions that there was no room in the inn.

For many people at St Andrew's there was an absence of any sense of real belonging, purpose or value: it was turn up, sit down and go home. It was possible to go for months and successfully avoid speaking to anybody. And that might be funny, except that for many people it was also very painful and so they left in large numbers.

The effect of all this was to turn a congregation into an audience. Consumerism had come creeping in and very nearly consumed us. To quote Erwin McManus in *An Unstoppable Force*, whereas we should have been saying, 'We are the church and we are here to serve a lost and broken world,' the mantra was increasingly, 'What does the church have to offer me?' or in other words, 'If you want my patronage you had better cater to my tastes and needs.'

This consumerism was also greedy to be fed with professionalism. I love excellence. I enjoy a job well done, and anybody who has ever worked with me will tell you that seven years as a litigator have made me really picky. But this all-consuming demand for professionalism was having a catastrophic effect on the release of our people's many gifts. As we raised excellence as a value (and we could put on a show!), so we diminished the desire and the opportunity for our people to explore and grow in their gifting: 'Everything here is done so professionally, so why would you need me?' At the same time, if you did have a leadership gifting your options were narrowed to leading a small group or getting ordained.

There was also a growing sense of disconnectedness. A recurring complaint was, 'I just don't know anybody.' This had serious and damaging consequences for the life of the church, because if people feel they don't belong they don't invite and they won't contribute.

And the overwhelming tragedy in all of this was that the congregation at St Andrew's Chorleywood was a gold reserve. The level of gifting and maturity within the congregation was staggering. Here was a congregation whose historic roots had ushered renewal into the UK and into the Anglican stream, had pioneered New Wine and planted Soul Survivor Watford. Mark's ministry had continued in this apostolic vein, raising up prophets, teachers, pastors and preachers. We were rich with leaders. Again, thanks to Mark's courageous use of the 'E' word (evangelism) there was also a very keen sense of what we needed to do with all that gifting and experience – to be so filled with the Father's love that we can't resist giving it away. But how were we going to do that? My interview presentation seemed puny by comparison with the enormity of the problem. I was at least clear that small groups alone were not the remedy.

The Val Doonican Christmas Special

If small groups alone were not the solution, what about our missional potency as a gathered congregation? That Christmas there was another sobering moment. As for many churches, Christmas was a great opportunity for us to encourage those who would not ordinarily attend church to step across our threshold. So the machinery was cranked up to put together a seeker-sensitive carol service par excellence. These were the days before our refurbishment, and if truth be told, we were looking a little threadbare in places. St Andrew's had worked very hard over its history and the building was looking a little battle weary. There is a somewhat derisive line in the novel *Barchester Towers* where Trollope describes the bishop's palace. He carefully records that it all looked truly sumptuous – or at least it would by candlelight. And that was us. Turn on the lights and it was bald brown carpet and crusty wicker lampshades – turn the lights down and light a few candles and we were Val Doonican's Christmas Special on ice!

I have never seen so many candles. You could have read our pew leaflets from outer space with the amount of candlelight we poured over this event. We had the biggest Christmas tree we could get into the church, magnificently decorated in co-ordinating Christmas colours (none of your cotton wool snowmen on this tree). We brought in The King's Chamber Orchestra – a nineteen-piece Christian orchestra – all of whom were world-class musicians. And to top it all off we invited a guest speaker. The orchestra drew us into heavenly places in our carolling. Our guest speaker was outstanding. It was a triumph. We were packed out at both services.

And at both services we made an invitation for people to come forward to give their lives to Jesus – and at both services they stayed in their seats in their hundreds. Not because they had not been moved. Not because they did not think that this was the best seeker-sensitive carol service they had ever been to. The problem was that they were already Christians. The big tragic irony was that at the end of our church driveway there were hundreds of thousands of people who did not know the Lord, while within we had successfully brought together a few hundred who did. Most of them sat there and commented, 'Goodness, my not-yet-Christian neighbours would have loved this.' We will never know if that was true, because the not-yet-Christian neighbours were at a very safe distance. I remember standing at the back in my new suit and thinking it would have been better to send these people out carol-singing. How many communities had we successfully emptied of their local mission potential that night?

So there was a lot to think about. There was also an increasing pressure building. In the October that preceded this Christmas extravaganza, I overheard Mark addressing the Sunday congregation. With tremendous conviction he assured them, '. . . and in two weeks' time (which happened to be 5 November) at a special mid-week meeting, Andrew will be bringing us the new strategy for local mission and small groups.' Just for added adrenal emphasis he added, 'This is going to be a very important evening and I would like everybody to be there.' I think my face drained of all blood. The fuse paper had just been lit, I had just two weeks and I had almost absolutely nothing.

3

UNLOCKING THE GOLD RESERVE

Andrew Williams

I had two weeks and one vaguely original thought. This would not be the first time in this saga that I felt overwhelmed with the vastness of the task. I came into my office on the following Monday and reread my interview presentation, hoping for a bit of fresh inspiration. There in the text was buried the idea that a group of Christians larger than a small group but not as large as the whole congregation might just be the way forward. I remember thinking that if this really was the Lord's plan then he would have to give me a pretty big green light; it felt like a giant button to push. By this time Mark had filled me in with some more recent St Andrew's history, during which the church had flirted with other cell and small group strategies. St Andrew's did not need any more false starts.

I put my paper to one side and started opening my post. Among my papers was a flyer for an event at St Thomas' Crookes in Sheffield. Mark had obviously seen this and in his familiar script he had written across the top, 'Drew, is this of any use to you?' The flyer described a conference looking at the growth of St Thomas' through the development of 'clusters'. Even from the face of the flyer I could see that their strategy was built around some of the principles that I had been mulling over. I was relieved. My one original thought might not be entirely original, but at least there was a source of wisdom and experience that I could build on. I was dancing around my office waving the flyer in my hand and thanking the Lord in what was a Davidic moment of indignity when my eyes fell on the date of the conference: it was 6 December. That was no good to me. I had to reorganise the universe by 5 November. I stopped dancing.

Fortunately I had a legal training and I knew what to do. I would make a phone call standing up. This always worked. Somehow 'standing up' phone calls carry that extra bit of gravitas – or at least someone had told me that once, and they were probably standing up when they said it, so I had believed them. I would stand up and call St Thomas' Crookes and I would tell them that I was the associate vicar of St Andrew's Chorleywood and ask if they would see me. In an upright position, shoulders back, head held high, I left a pleading message on the telephone answering machine of Bob and Mary Hopkins.

Bob and Mary Hopkins are on the staff at St Thomas' and head up Anglican Church Planting Initiatives. They are very good people. One day, when the books on revival in the twenty-first century are written, some tenacious historian is suddenly going to realise that the Lord rebuilt his church in the United Kingdom through a great deal of their blood, sweat and tears. They were very kind and got back to me via my assistant Judith. Their message read, 'Good to hear from you. Hope you are settling in well at Chorleywood. Sorry – can't meet with you until January.' Had I not sufficiently explained

my dilemma? Had they not heard that I was standing up
when I made that call? Did they not realise that the
world was going to end on 5 November? I then plagued
them with phone calls – standing up, sitting down,
kneeling, prostrate, I tried it all. Eventually Bob weak-
ened. He called me and said, 'Look, you are clearly very
keen to meet with us. Our diaries are full but we can
give you a half-hour telephone conference.' Before I had
time to think, my response was out: 'Bob, that is so kind
of you and Mary. If you will give me a thirty-minute
phone call I will drive to Sheffield so that I can at least be
sitting in front of you for the duration of that half-hour.'
He said he would call me back. The message came: 'We
surrender. See you Thursday at the Philadelphia
Campus – midday.' There was the sound of a little more
Davidic dancing but not too much; it was now Friday
and I had just ten days left before the end of the world.

Another Caesar salad

I always hesitate to say that I am a Devonian, because I
was not born in Devon and people who were do not take
kindly to you taking that sort of liberty. But I did do a lot
of growing up in the West Country. So for me,
Chorleywood was already an extreme northerly out-
post. If you grow up in a place like Tavistock, places like
Exeter and Okehampton are cosmopolitan jungles. I
took my driving test in a town called Launceston, where
there were no roundabouts or traffic lights or indeed
very much traffic but there were lots of hazardous
sheep. I mention this because in all the drama I realised
that I had no idea where Sheffield was, save that it must
be up the M1 somewhere. I did a bit of research and
found out that the Philadelphia Campus was not in

south-east Pennsylvania but was in fact a disused industrial site on the outskirts of Sheffield from where Mike
Breen and his team were rebuilding the Kingdom of God
in the north. As I thought about it, the odds of me successfully locating Sheffield, navigating all those traffic
lights and roundabouts and then finding this disused
industrial site – all by midday – did not seem very high.
I was obviously a little bit fretful about this appointment, and the night before I was due to make the journey I had a very vivid dream. A very tall man, all
dressed in white, whose face was radiant and shining,
came to me and said, 'Do not fear, I will travel with you
to Sheffield.' Looking back now I can see the Lord's
encouragement and provision in that dream. I was in
such an anxious state, however, that even in my dream I
said to this figure, 'I can't take any passengers. I have
to be there by midday and I have no idea where I am
headed – you will have to get the bus!'

So the morning came. Elena had worked out a route
map for me (I even made her write it out backwards so that
I could find my way home) which was stuck to the dashboard. I was praying hard. My prayer was simple: 'Lord, if
what I am sensing is of you, please give me a green light.'
On the way up I thought I would raise my faith levels with
a new worship CD. It just annoyed the heck out of me. All
that joyful praising was really just too much. Anyway, I
found Sheffield (it is quite a large place, as it happens) and
made my way through the city. There were many roundabouts and a great number of traffic lights – all of which
were red. But clearly the big guy in the big white dress and
the big white smile was in the back seat or on the roof of
the car or somewhere, because at exactly midday I pulled
up outside the Philadelphia Campus.

It took a great deal of self-control to suppress a quick
chorus of 'I did it! I did it!' down the security intercom,

but I managed to compose myself and they let me in. Very shortly afterwards I was sitting in front of Bob Hopkins. The sun was behind him and I could see the vast industrial proportions of the Philadelphia Campus in the window immediately behind him. There was something rather Bond-like about the moment, and I half-expected Bob to have a cat on his lap. He did not have a cat, but as he sat in his swivel chair, for a moment, his demeanour was just a little bit Goldfinger. He was very gracious but very clear. 'Okay, you have called this meeting – what do you want to say to us?'

It poured out of me. I think that I spoke without pausing for about twenty minutes. Looking back, that might have been a big mistake, because they had only promised me thirty! I told him how I now realised that I was one in a long line of noble men who had been tasked with sorting out small groups at St Andrew's and that so far nothing had turned it around. I told him how I was not convinced that small groups were the right vehicle for mission and that I had a gut sense that we needed to mobilise a new sort of group, a sort of mid-sized community, bigger than a small group but smaller than the congregation. I told him about the gold reserve – about the latent gifting that was ready to be released. I shared with him my anxieties about the attractional model; that the 'come to us' paradigm was failing us. I finished by saying, 'We need to mobilise the Lord's army and get them out of the barracks.' Bob smiled. His response was completely unexpected. He said, 'Would you like to ghost-write my next book?' His face was beaming and I knew that the Lord was sitting in on this meeting. He went on, 'I believe that you are right,' and with characteristic humility he added, 'I believe that we might be able to help you. Let's all go and get something to eat.'

Over a very good Caesar salad, it transpired that while I had been in the process of coming to faith, being baptised in the Spirit, giving up law, getting ordained etc., St Thomas' had been rebuilding the Kingdom of God with a model they referred to as 'clusters'. These clusters were built upon many of the values that I had been rather amateurishly pondering. I mentioned to Bob that St Andrew's had already used the word 'cluster' for another venture that had not gone so well. Bob was very matter-of-fact: 'You will have to come up with something else.' In a moment that did not feel especially significant I threw out, 'Well, something like "mid-sized community" would do it.' Bob laughed and immediately saw the abbreviation: MSC – MISSION-SHAPED CHURCH.

On the back of a napkin I scribbled away as Bob and Mary poured out a lot of wisdom. They said many things over that lunch, but there were three things that would serve us well over the next few months. Each mid-sized community must have three things. Firstly, it must have a clear mission purpose. That could be any number of things – a neighbourhood, age group, interest group etc. Secondly, it must have a name that captured the essence of its mission purpose. And thirdly, an MSC, led by a leadership team from within the congregation, must not be bigger than sixty adult members (we have since revised this to fifty but this was our starting point). Once it came close to reaching that number it must multiply.

I certainly got a lot more than thirty minutes from them, and with the napkin in my pocket we said our farewells and I headed back to Chorleywood. As I made my way through Sheffield I was playing the new worship CD very loudly and every traffic light that I came to was green.

I managed to decipher Elena's homebound directions and in what felt like no time at all I was back in Chorleywood. Generally I don't like to bother Mark at the vicarage, but the napkin was burning a hole in my pocket. He was seated at the kitchen table, painting toy soldiers with Sam. I waved the napkin and said, 'I think I may just have something.'

Remember, remember

So the end of the world as we knew it arrived and a large number of the congregation turned out to see what the brave new church might look like. I took my place at the podium and, having polished up the scribbles on the napkin, proceeded to set out the strategy. St Andrew's is at the bottom of a lot of people's gardens in Chorleywood. This particular night it was evident that the neighbours had entered a pyrotechnic competition. Never before or after has Guy Fawkes Night been celebrated with such gusto and such vast quantities of gunpowder. It was trench warfare, cannon to the left and cannon to the right. It felt as though I was preaching from the Somme. The old crusty wicker lampshades were shaking in their sockets and depositing forty-year-old debris over our heads. What I had hoped would be a warm and inviting casting of a vision became a battle-cry. The Lord does work in mysterious ways.

As if the fireworks were not enough, I shared a shocking true story that went something like this:

> In a place that is not unknown to me there is a scattering of small churches, each with tiny congregations of about eight to twelve people who say, 'We may be small but we are perfect. We like things just the way they are and we

think we have just enough in us to continue in this way until we die.' The sad fact is that they are absolutely correct and when they die the church in that community will die with them. These congregations have succumbed to the temptation to withdraw from the world, to pull up the drawbridge and join the heritage industry.

One of these churches had some building works carried out for a few months and so it was necessary for the small congregation to meet for Sunday morning worship in the village hall. Over this period the congregation of eight began to grow. Somehow the warm but tatty informality of the community hall was attractive to those who would not brave the bevelled pew. There was space for children, and some new families joined them each Sunday. A widower out walking his dog one Sunday morning was curious to find out where all the singing was coming from and he felt so welcome that he and his dog became regular members. The congregation trebled in this season out of its building. The original eight church members were taken by surprise and called an emergency meeting of the church council. As they were all on the church council this was not difficult to arrange. And the main item on the top of their agenda was how they would go back to their church building without taking the new people with them.

There were a few gasps. It was a shocking story, but to allow our local mission to continue on its current trajectory was to take us dangerously close to this precipice. Over the fireworks I told them that I believed it was God's desire to breathe new life into our small-group work to reverse the decline. What I wanted to do that evening was to cast a new strategy, and I wanted the church to get excited about the possibilities.

Moving to the far side of the platform, I affirmed the place of the small group as a setting that provided more intimate fellowship and pastoral care, a sense of belonging, discipleship, an opportunity to study the Word of God and a midweek opportunity for worship and prayer. Walking across to the other side of the platform, I then affirmed the larger Sunday gathering. Here was a place where we might all have sight of God's greatness, a time to stand shoulder to shoulder with the Lord's people and enter into grand and glorious worship, a place of larger belonging and leading, where corporate vision and strategy were communicated and values, beliefs and ethos were established. But between the big and the small (I now raced to the middle of the platform and jumped up and down for extra emphasis) there was something to be rediscovered. Somewhere between the small group and the large Sunday gathering, the Lord was calling us to pioneer lay-led mission-shaped communities. I outlined ten key principles (you will recognise the first three from the napkin):

A mid-sized (or mission-shaped) community (MSC):

1. has its own distinct vision for mission – for example by age group, neighbourhood, network or some other specific area of common interest.
2. has a name – key to building identity and belonging.
3. is a community of up to sixty adults who regularly meet together. [This was our starting point in 2003. Today we put a ceiling of up to fifty adults, which we have found serves the mission and purpose of the MSC a lot better.]
4. is led by members of the church family – preferably with a leadership team.
5. seeks to identify emerging leaders.

6. is committed to forming new small groups from within its membership that share its distinct vision for mission.
7. has a heart to see the MSC multiply – so that when it reaches sixty adult members it multiplies to create another MSC from within its membership.
8. is accountable to the sending church and its ordained leadership (to quote Mike Breen, this strategy was low on control but high on accountability).
9. remains part of the gathered church.
10. is 'lightweight'/inexpensive/not bound by building or maintenance.

I also emphasised that within the wide parameters of the strategy this was a bottom-up model. At its roots this strategy asked a question and then gave permission. The critical first question was always, 'What is the Lord saying to you?' In other words, what are you passionate about? What makes you weep as you watch the news? Where do you want to make a difference? The permission was simply a question of how we could support a church member in making that passion a reality. So how an MSC came into being, how often it met, where it met – all of these decisions were worked out prayerfully in accordance with its mission.

I wanted so much to put the adventure back into the Christian venture. With all my heart I wanted this strategy to get people excited again about what it is to follow Jesus and to watch him open doors and hearts before their eyes. I was passionate to see the release of the gold reserve – to liberate and refine the substantial latent gifting within the body of Christ. I longed to see this strategy release vision, innovation and creativity and enable the church to grow in faith and serve in mission with greater confidence and capacity.

I finished with these thoughts: 'I know there are many questions that all this raises. I hope you can see that at the core of this strategy is our working these questions out together with our Heavenly Father. Let me tell you what this model is not about. This is not about the church demanding more time during the week but a more creative way of using the time we offer. This is not about the imposition of a structure but about empowering vision and releasing gifts. I remain firmly of the view that God has placed a very high calling on the life of his church. I believe that this is a new season in God, a season of harvest. I believe the Lord is lining us up to go out into the harvest fields, to give away his heart all over again. We are to have a new commissioning, a fresh anointing as the older brother. I believe that it is time to break open the gold reserves.'

There was some applause, and from the back someone cheered and said, 'Amen'. I was really encouraged by that. More importantly, there was an all-night prayer meeting directly afterwards and I was humbled to see so many people piling into the chapel, and our intercessory leaders, Helen Clark and her wonderful late husband Phil, on their knees, leading our people in prayer for the realisation of the strategy. There was a conviction and a hunger in their prayers that convinced me something important had just happened.

The Rossers

One of the difficult questions was what to do with the existing small-group network. I was reluctant to disband it but I wanted to give our people some freedom, to expand their horizons. So I declared an open season. What I meant by that was that everyone had the opportunity for a fresh start. If a church member had been part of a small group for many years and was wondering if there was any way out but by death, then this was their opportunity for life in the land of the living, to quote Psalm 27. This seemed to go down quite well. From one small group six people came forward who in the fullness of time all went on to become MSC leaders.

Two of these were David and Jenny Rosser. In my humble opinion, when you look at some of the most significant things that God has done with his church in this country over the past thirty years or so, you won't have to look too hard before you find David and Jenny labouring away in the background. Long before a lot of people see what is going on, David and Jenny are there serving; faithfully fanning embers into flame. For thirty years or more David and Jenny have been in the Christian publishing industry, and they have been members at St Andrew's for almost twenty years. If you go anywhere at all with David and Jenny they will always know someone. Whatever the event, however remote, whatever time of the day; from Sheffield to the Shetlands, Bracknell to Boston, in the queue, on the conference platform, behind the resources table, they will know someone. Actually it is invariably two people, and the chances are they published a book for one of them.

I did not know any of that the day they came to see me with a proposal. The fireworks were over, and on a dank and dreary November afternoon they sat down in my office. Jenny began, 'We have listened to your strategy and we have been waiting for this for seven years.' If truth be told, that alone would have made my day, but then they really surprised me. David stroked his famous moustache, looked me straight between the eyes and said, 'We think that this is going to be very big and you cannot do this on your own. We will come and give you one day a week and we will do whatever is needed.' It was love at first sight. There was a part of me that was wondering if they wouldn't mind repeating what they had just said so that I could write it down and then have them sign it. But their word was their bond – except that one day a week became eight days a week.

The yeast in the dough

The Lord had shown me that he would raise up twelve people to pioneer this work. At that time the congregation was about six hundred people, so possibly this does not sound especially generous or faithful, but Bob and Mary had assured me that once we got the yeast in the dough the miracle of multiplication would follow. Twelve was a great promise from the Lord. At the vision-casting night on 5 November I had invited any early pioneers to join me for a meeting on 6 December to pilot a few MSCs. My hope was that we would feed back to the church, by way of testimony, the goodness of what was going on and encourage others to get involved.

By now David and Jenny were part of the team with Judith and me. On that Saturday morning we stood together in the chapel and prayed in the twelve. And in they came. What was even more spectacular was that as they shared their hearts, albeit tentatively at the start, we began to see sovereign connections take place within the group. Across the room people found that they had come with the same passion; MSC leadership teams were coalescing before our very eyes.

From this meeting came some highly innovative outreach. Before long we had some pilot MSCs that each carried their own distinct mission. They were wonderfully diverse and their mission brief arose from the hearts of those the Lord called to lead them. An MSC was established in the local library under the title TGIB (Thank God It's Bedtime), which was an MSC with a heart to reach young parents and give them parenting skills. It was tremendously successful. Although TGIB was relatively short-lived, there is one young mum who attended that MSC who has now committed her life to the Lord and is part of a thriving MSC within her community. TGIB was her lifeline. Another MSC recognised that there were many people living in the area from overseas who would appreciate the opportunity to come together and be community. Friends International did a wonderful job in drawing together some very lonely people within the love of God.

All of this was fed back to the church. The abbreviation MSC, first scribbled on the back of a napkin in a café in Sheffield, was becoming part of the language of the church. I think if I had realised how quickly the yeast was going to spread I might have tried to come up with something a bit more elegant. One of my lecturers from theological college bumped into me at about this time and asked what I was up to. I told him the story thus far and he grunted, 'The name is awful.' I think he was probably right, but it was spreading so fast we did not have time for much finesse.

Open Door

One of the first larger MSCs was Open Door. This was developed out of a number of small groups which had a heart to reach a particular neighbourhood just outside Watford. I have some very special memories of how this all came about. On one occasion, David, Jenny and I were visiting one of the existing small groups, and for what felt like the umpteenth time for me I was taking them through the strategy. I was not sure how well I was being received, but then without notice a fine white smoke filled the room; I thought it was condensation. Through the cloud, Trevor (the group leader) beamed at me and said, 'We're in!' It was only in the car on the way home that we realised that quite possibly the Lord had revealed his purposes in a particularly glorious way.

I recall so clearly going along to one of the first Open Door meetings. They had prayed and the Lord had led them to a community hall in the local area. It was a simple building with a public bar at one end and our new MSC in a room at the other end. It was now early spring and people were working on the allotments that surrounded the community hall. Our guys began to worship, and as they did you could see many people on their allotments stop work and stand and listen. The floor in the hall was sticky underfoot from all the spilled beer and you could hear a CD player belting out a Michael Jackson song, 'You are not alone.' As our group continued in worship, I noticed that the music was turned off so that they could listen. As we have continued in this work our MSCs have been inspired to do many things to get alongside the people in the bars and on the allotments. Open Door multiplied to become three MSCs in due course. Tonight, however, was a declaration of the Lord's intent. Here was a tangible expression of all that we had longed and prayed for taking shape. I went home and sent Mark an email: 'Whatever anybody may say, I know what I saw tonight and what I saw was fire break out at Open Door.'

On the home front

On the home front, perhaps not surprisingly, this was not an easy time for us as a family. Elena was taken ill in the middle of the night. She had gone to bed feeling unwell and at about 2.00 in the morning I awoke to see her pacing the floor and holding her stomach. At about 3.15 she was really very ill, and when she told me that she would rather be giving birth I realised that we should definitely call the doctor. Two hours later Elena was taken by ambulance to the accident and emergency unit at Watford Hospital.

If you have never been to the emergency unit at Watford Hospital, let me tell you it's nothing like the American TV series *ER*, and not a lot like *Casualty* either. Decoratively it is much more like *Coronation Street* – but without the technology and glamour. They hide you in little curtained booths and you wait for someone to come and find you. I put my head on the side of Elena's trolley bed, and when the doctor arrived I was aware that I had been asleep with my mouth open and had been dribbling. The doctor asked Elena if she might be pregnant. Elena said, 'Definitely not,' and I said, 'Well, there might be an outside chance.' They both took a sideways look at me with dribble running down my chin and the doctor said, 'So we can rule out pregnancy.'

In another booth very near to us we could hear quite a bit of commotion coming through the curtains. There was a young man who would have been in a lot of pain had he been sober. Through the curtain it became clear that he had been involved in a fight with someone who had tried to bite both his ears off. The nurses were keen to wake him up and get him to the plastic surgery unit. And there followed a surreal conversation about where they had put his shoes and his trousers. This went on for some time. Everyone in the hospital was looking for this guy's trousers. They never found them. Elena was being really sick on one side of the curtain and on the other side there was this pitiable young man with no ears and

no trousers shuffling past in just his socks. It was such a
tragic and broken image. I prayed, 'Lord in all this darkness, I can't see you.' I did at least have the presence of
mind to pray for the young man, and as I prayed for him
I heard the ambulance driver say with such compassion,
'Here, son, let me put this blanket around you.' There in
all the darkness was the Father's voice. I think what really struck me that night was the urgency of our getting
out of the church and into this dark world with the
Father's love. This was not a game. This was a battle.

Praying for dynamite

And so we battled on. They were not able to diagnose
Elena properly at that point and we had several more
visits to the hospital over the coming months. But in
this season we established seventeen MSCs, and four
hundred church members left the cruise ship to man
the lifeboats. We now had forty new MSC leaders,
many of them leading groups for the first time. At this
time these were all midweek MSCs. And this was all
very good. And yet I had a nagging concern that this
was just not enough. Many of our new MSCs were outside Chorleywood. Not surprisingly, some of the
church family needed a little more convincing. They
were always very gracious with me. Nevertheless, I
could see that I was fast becoming something of an irri-
tant and to be perfectly honest, I was really beginning
to irritate myself. Someone said to me recently that at
that time if they had heard me say 'MSC' just one more
time they would have thumped me. I felt exactly the
same.

I recall praying one afternoon in advance of a meeting
with a group of local small-group leaders. David and

Jenny were with me in this prayer time, and as we pleaded with the Lord to move the mission of the church forward the Lord drew my attention to Revelation 14:2–3: 'And I heard a sound from heaven like the roar of rushing waters and like a loud peal of thunder. The sound I heard was like that of harpists playing their harps. And they sang a new song before the throne . . .'

As I read this verse, the sky broke open with thunder. It was so loud it made me jump. I recall my prayer: 'O Lord, won't you put some dynamite under this strategy?' Be very careful what you pray for.

4

FINDING THE DYNAMITE

Mark Stibbe

Not long ago, *USA Today* – one of America's leading daily newspapers – published a great story entitled 'Super Granny: Defender of Justice'. It read as follows:

> An elderly Florida lady did her shopping, and upon returning to her car, she found four males in the act of leaving with her vehicle. She dropped her shopping bags and drew her handgun, proceeding to scream at the top of her voice 'I have a gun, and I know how to use it. Get out of the car!'
>
> The four men didn't wait for a second invitation. They got out and ran like mad. The lady, somewhat shaken, then proceeded to load her shopping bags into the back of the car and get into the driver's seat. She was so shaken that she could not get her key into the ignition.
>
> She tried and tried, and then it dawned on her why. A few minutes later she found her own car parked four or five spaces farther down. She loaded her bags into the car and then drove to the police station.
>
> The sergeant to whom she told the story doubled over on the floor with laughter. He pointed to the other end of the counter, where four pale men were reporting a car

jacking by a mad, elderly woman described as white, less than five feet tall, glasses, curly white hair, and carrying a large handgun.

No charges were filed. . . .

The moral of this story – or at least one of the morals of this story – is, 'It's important to find the right vehicle!'

A brand new vehicle

Drew Williams' arrival at St Andrew's Chorleywood provided the creativity we were looking for in the implementation of our vision. As I showed in Chapter 1, the vision was clear right from the start of my time at St Andrew's. My very first sermon was based on the call of the Bridegroom in Song of Songs 2:8–13. From the beginning of 1997 we knew where we were heading – outwards in mission to the lost. What we hadn't clearly seen was exactly how to get there.

After Drew's first six months we began to see that the Holy Spirit was leading us to form brand new vehicles for our mission. We had spent years looking at other churches and movements throughout the world, and we had tried using some of their vehicles for our own mission. In the end we realised that the Lord wanted to create something new, something that would grow out of the soil of St Andrew's Chorleywood, not out of someone else's experience. The MSCs were the innovative vehicles that grew organically out of the ground of our own pursuit of God.

It is really important at this point to say two things about these mid-sized communities. First of all, MSCs are not the same as what are sometimes referred to as 'clusters'. As we understand it, clusters are often just that – clusters. They are groups of small groups that form together into a larger group of anything up to one hundred people. In the cluster model, very often it is the small groups that form first and then these cells cluster together into a larger grouping. Diagrammatically this looks as follows:

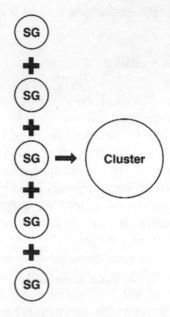

In the cluster model, the small groups come first and the medium-size group comes second, arising out of the small groups.

In the MSC model, the mid-sized community is the starting point. A group of twenty to thirty people get together with a shared vision for outreach and form an MSC. As they begin that work, they recognise the need to meet in smaller groups that meet different needs – needs for pastoral care, prayer ministry, deeper study of the Word, and so on. Diagrammatically this looks as follows:

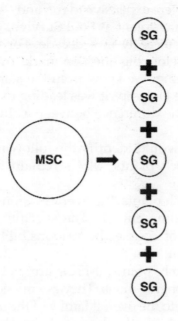

The difference between MSCs and clusters is quite marked. In the cluster model, the cell or small group is the primary building block for mission. In the MSC model, the MSC is the primary building block for mission. The MSC is built first, and then small groups flow naturally out of it.

A second point to make is that there is a big difference between MSCs and church plants. Our MSCs were never designed as independent church plants but rather as inter-dependent missional communities. In fact, we were convinced from the start that church planting was not the way for us to go. We had three church plants already at St Andrew's and we could see from their experience that they were very different from what we were creating. In many ways our church plants were clones of the sending church, imitating almost exactly the worship style and patterns of St Andrew's Church. In addition, they required paid staff and were expensive to run and – with the exception of our church plant at Soul Survivor Watford – had not grown significantly in a decade. For Drew and me, there were therefore big question marks over conventional church planting. We knew from the start that this was not the way the Holy Spirit was leading us to go.

So what is the difference between a church plant and an MSC?

Drew and I would identify the following differences.

Unlike church plants, MSCs remain integral to the sending church.

Unlike church plants, the overall vision for the MSC is set by the sending church. The specific outworking of that vision is of course the responsibility of the MSC leadership team.

Unlike church plants, MSCs are not independent, autonomous congregations. They are missional communities that belong to the overall family of the sending church.

Unlike church plants, the people involved in an MSC are first and foremost members of the sending church, not the MSC

Unlike church plants, MSCs are highly mobile, able to uproot from the places where they meet at a moment's notice.

Unlike church plants, the leaders of MSCs are not paid but are entirely voluntary, as is everyone else.

Unlike church plants, MSCs are not financially independent but give their tithes to the sending church.

Unlike church plants, new converts in an MSC are baptised by immersion at the sending church, not in the MSC itself.

Unlike church plants, MSCs cannot grow beyond fifty adult members but have to multiply into a new MSC when they reach that ceiling.

Unlike church plants, MSCs are called to reproduce new missional communities.

Unlike church plants, MSCs do not meet every Sunday but return to the sending church on the fourth Sunday of each month.

Unlike church plants, MSCs use Bible teaching provided by the sending church (by Drew and me) and used by every other MSC.

Unlike church plants, MSCs are mandated to teach the Word in unconventional ways, using an interactive learning process. In other words, those tasked with teaching in the MSCs are urged to find creative ways of involving their audience in studying God's Word.

Unlike church plants, MSCs are resourced primarily by the sending church, not by themselves.

These are just some of the main differences between an MSC and a traditional church plant. It is important to stress these differences and to be clear about them. When Drew found the right vehicle for the outworking of our vision it was not something borrowed or imported but something given by revelation of the Holy Spirit. To be sure, Drew interacted with other mission-shaped models of church growth in the process of this discovery. Bob and Mary Hopkins were especially invaluable in helping us to see the exact contours of the new vehicle that the Father was giving to us. But this was not, I stress, something acquired from a conference, a book or another ministry. This was the Father's gift to us for the next season of our church's life and growth, and we were thankful.

A glorious morning in June

In the weeks from November 2003 to June 2004, Drew and his team were piloting the first of the MSCs and had

managed to woo four hundred members of our church
into midweek communities. This in itself was an outstanding achievement. But Drew – feeling that this was
not the beginning of the end, but the end of the beginning – had prayed for the Holy Spirit to put dynamite
underneath the work. And that is precisely what happened next.

The dynamite showed up in an unexpected guise.
While we had been moving our church members into
MSCs, we had also been in a process of discussion about
our main facility, the St Andrew's Church building.
When I had arrived in 1997 I had felt strongly that the
building was sub-standard for our missional purposes
and that it was showing all the signs of being tired and
tatty. Apart from anything else, I felt that this could not
be left indefinitely without it starting to become dis-
honouring to the Lord. So I had agreed with the PCC
that we would refurbish the building and in 2003 had
mandated a sub-group of the PCC to begin the planning.

By May 2003 it had become clear that the refurbishment would not be a quick, three-week clean-up (which
we had originally anticipated) but rather a nine-month
upheaval. Indeed, we were told that we would have to
be out of the building in September, and that the
builders and their diggers would be coming in and we
would all have to meet somewhere else. This concentrated our minds so powerfully that I felt it necessary to
call an emergency staff away-day at Latimer in June
2003 in order to plan how we would function as a church
without our building.

And so it was that we gathered together in a large
room in the glorious setting of the Chess Valley on a
swelteringly hot summer's day. Over twenty staff team
members arrived, including Drew in his brand new blue
vehicle (which, to this day, he regards as prophetic in

itself). We spent about an hour worshipping the Father and there was a very strong sense of the presence of God in the room. As we worshipped the Lord, Drew had a vision in which he saw Peter stepping out of the boat and walking on water. It was so strong that Drew actually spoke it out. One member of the staff then read the passage to us from Matthew 14:22–33:

> *Immediately Jesus made the disciples get into the boat and go on ahead of him to the other side, while he dismissed the crowd. After he had dismissed them, he went up on a mountainside by himself to pray. When evening came, he was there alone, but the boat was already a considerable distance from land, buffeted by the waves because the wind was against it.*
>
> *During the fourth watch of the night Jesus went out to them, walking on the lake. When the disciples saw him walking on the lake, they were terrified. 'It's a ghost,' they said, and cried out in fear*
>
> *But Jesus immediately said to them: 'Take courage! It is I. Don't be afraid.'*
>
> *'Lord, if it's you,' Peter replied, 'tell me to come to you on the water.'*
>
> *'Come,' he said.*
>
> *Then Peter got down out of the boat, walked on the water and came towards Jesus. But when he saw the wind, he was afraid and, beginning to sink, cried out, 'Lord, save me!' Immediately Jesus reached out his hand and caught him. 'You of little faith,' he said, 'why did you doubt?'*
>
> *And when they climbed into the boat, the wind died down. Then those who were in the boat worshipped him, saying, 'Truly you are the Son of God.'*

As the time of worship drew to a close, I gathered my thoughts together in preparation for the discussion. The first question on the agenda, which was really the one big question for the day, was this: 'What are we going to do without a building?' As everyone sat down around several very large round tables, I posed the question, waiting to hear not only what my staff were saying but more importantly, what the Holy Spirit was about to say through them. The first answer that was given was that we should hire the biggest hall in Chorleywood – a concert hall at the local comprehensive school – and meet there every Sunday for celebration events. After five minutes it seemed that this was the answer. Anticipating this prospect, I had already asked my then PA, Missie, to investigate the cost of that hall and pencil in the bookings.

However, at this point something happened that turned the whole discussion around. One member of the staff piped up with the following comment: 'I don't think that's the answer. I believe that the MSCs which Drew has been developing are the way forward. I sense the Lord is calling all of us to get out of the boat and walk on water. The whole church is to get into MSCs.'

I remember at this moment thinking, 'That's not what I want to do in the flesh. I like big celebrations. It would be fun to speak to everyone in one place.' But in my spirit, the Holy Spirit was saying, 'What you have just heard is the truth.' So I turned to Drew and asked him what he thought. Drew's recollection of this moment is that he felt it was not feasible in human terms to get everyone into MSCs. To be honest, he felt we were not strong enough to orchestrate such a massive logistical operation. But then, in his own words, Drew felt the Holy Spirit giving him a 'kick up the backside' and he heard the Lord say to him, 'This is me.' And Drew then said, 'We have to do this.' All I remember is that at that moment everyone agreed with sudden conviction and unity that this was the way to go, and I remember seeing

Drew putting his head in his hands and saying to himself, 'Oh no, what have I just said?' Another member of staff said these very telling words: 'If we can really do this it will change everything.' Another said, 'We must do it, but we mustn't dilute what the Lord is saying to us in any way.' That morning was the morning when everything changed. The dynamite was being prepared.

A party for prostitutes

The rest of the morning was taken up with planning the move out of the building and the shape of our monthly Sunday programme. Initially there was a suggestion that we should meet all together in the concert hall on three Sundays a month, and out in the MSCs one Sunday. But then we realised that this would be diluting the vision and we had been expressly warned not to do that, so we felt it right to reverse that plan and meet out in our MSCs three Sundays a month, and in the concert hall on the fourth. On the fourth Sunday we would have a morning and evening celebration, I would preach on the vision and Drew would interview people from our MSCs so that testimonies could be shared.

As we broke for lunch there was a rising sense of excitement and expectation among the staff. By the end of the lunch break we had reached a strong consensus on the way forward, so we changed direction for the afternoon session from 2.00 to 4.00 pm. I had felt it right to share a talk with the staff that afternoon, in preparation for a presentation I was due to give in September. The September appointment was a Saturday conference in a London church in which I had the opportunity of sharing the stage with Rowan Williams, the Archbishop of Canterbury, in a debate about the church. This was a critical time for the Church of England. There had been a great deal of controversy over the issue of homosexuality, and the Anglican Church in the UK was heading closer to schism. My task in the day was to present a Charismatic perspective on the issues.

That afternoon I gave the paper a trial run with my staff. I spoke on the subject of the church and the Kingdom of God. I spoke about two dimensions of Jesus' teaching on the Kingdom – hospitality and holiness. The essence of my message was that the Kingdom is an open set in which all are welcome and no one is turned away. But it is also a place of radical life change, where all who enter in are called to place every aspect of their lives under God's rule and lordship. My argument was that the local church is supposed to mirror these two aspects of the Kingdom. Every local church is called to embrace the dynamic marriage of inclusion and transformation. We are called to be inclusive and invitational, but we are also called to repentance and holiness. Jesus calls us all with the words, 'You can come as you are, but you cannot stay as you have been.'

In presenting this paper to the staff I told two stories. I told a story of a friend who is a senior pastor of a vibrant inner-city church. He was formerly a promiscuous homosexual involved in the gay scene. But he had encountered Jesus, had become a Christian, and over a period of time had come to a place of radical transformation.

In addition, I told a story narrated frequently by a Christian sociologist by the name of Dr Tony Campolo. On one occasion Tony flew from the United States to Honolulu. Because of the jet lag he woke at 3 o'clock in the morning with his body thinking it was 9 o'clock and time for breakfast. He got up, and wandered down the street from the hotel into a restaurant – a rather grotty, dirty place. He ordered a cup of coffee and a doughnut.

The man behind the counter was an unkempt individual named Harry. Harry handed Tony a doughnut. While he was drinking and eating, the door burst open and eight or nine boisterous prostitutes came in. They sat down at the counter next to Tony.

One of the women said, 'Tomorrow is my birthday. I'll be 39.' Her friend said, 'So what do you want from me? I suppose you want a party or something. Maybe you want me to bake you a cake.'

The first woman (who he later found out was named Agnes) said, 'Why are you so mean? I don't want anything from you. I've never had a birthday party and no one has ever baked me a cake. Be quiet!'

At that point Tony got an idea. When the ladies had left he said to Harry behind the counter, 'Do they come in here every night?'

'Yes, they do.'

'This one next to me – Agnes?'

'Same time, just like clockwork.'

So Tony said, 'What about if we throw a party for her, a birthday party?'

Harry began to smile and called to his wife. They agreed it was a wonderful idea and they made plans.

The next night Tony came back at the same time and the place was decorated with crepe paper and a sign on the wall which said, 'Happy Birthday, Agnes.' It had been cleaned up and looked like a different place. They sat down and waited. Soon others began to trickle in. Word had got round on the streets and prostitutes from all over Honolulu arrived.

At the regular time, Agnes and her friends burst through the door and everyone shouted, 'Happy birthday, Agnes!' Her knees buckled. Her friends caught her. She was stunned. They led her to the counter and she sat down. Harry brought the cake out, and her mouth fell open as her eyes filled with tears. They put the cake down in front of her and sang 'Happy birthday'.

Harry said, 'Blow the candles out so we can all have some.' But Agnes just stared at the cake. Finally they convinced her to blow out the candles. Harry handed her a knife and told her to cut the cake. She sat looking at the cake lovingly as if it was the most precious thing she had ever seen. Then she said, 'Do I have to cut it?'

Harry said, 'Well no, I suppose you don't have to cut it.'

Then she said something even more strange: 'I would like to keep it for a while. I don't live far from here. Can I take it home? I'll be right back.'

Everybody looked at her with puzzled faces and said, 'Sure, you can take it.'

She picked up the cake and carried it as if she was carrying the Holy Grail as she walked out the door.

There was stunned silence, then Tony Campolo started sharing with those left behind about Jesus. Harry said to him, 'Hey, I didn't know you were a preacher.'

Tony answered, 'I'm not a preacher. I'm a sociologist.'

Harry asked, 'Well, what kind of church do you come from anyway?'

Tony, inspired by God's Spirit, said, 'I guess I come from a church that throws birthday parties for prostitutes at 3 o'clock in the morning.'

And Harry said, 'No, you don't. There's no such church as that, 'cause if there was, I'd join it.'

Looking back on that sunny day in June, Drew would say that the afternoon was as important as the morning. In the morning we heard the call to break out of the box because the box (our building) was no longer going to be there. We heard the Holy Spirit's invitation to release God's people from one place and disperse them in missional communities in many different places – locations such as cafés, school halls, community centres, Scout headquarters, homeless shelters and so forth. In the afternoon I presented a vision of the local church as the expression of the expanding, growing reign of God in which all are welcome and everyone is transformed. I shared a picture of the church as a community of people that throws parties for prostitutes in cafés in the early hours of the morning.

Looking back, none of us realised how prophetic that was.

That was the week that was

Everyone left Latimer with a great sense of vision but also with a sober realisation of the work that needed to be done. Drew went straight home and sat in the garden with his assistants, David and Jenny Rosser, attending to the YBH factor. YBH stands for 'YES, BUT HOW?' Meanwhile, I went straight back to my desk at home to start planning for the week ahead. As I accessed my email to send some urgent messages, there was a message waiting for me from a student at London School of Theology, dated 5 June 2004, 4.29 pm. This is what it said:

> My name is Steve and I was in your evening service on Sunday 30 May when Mark was talking about Pentecost and the Holy Spirit doing a new thing. When we were all encouraged to pray and seek the Spirit, I felt that I had the following short picture for St Andrew's Church as a whole.
>
> It was a picture of a theatre. The audience was full and the stage had actors on it, but the whole picture was in greys and black. The show on stage was the last

performance of a long-running play and at the end of the performance there was a feeling of everything being tired out.

The final curtain (a black curtain) came down slowly; there was no applause and the whole picture went black. The picture then changed to the same theatre, but the stage curtain was now bright red and the whole theatre was bathed in bright light.

The curtains opened and the stage was full of colour and vibrant movement. I then noticed that no one was in the audience but everyone, audience and actors, was on stage, involved in the new play.

I just felt that I had to share this with you. I hope it is of some help. I have a few ideas about what it could mean but I will let you see what you make of it.

I was stunned. Steve knew nothing of our plans but he had seen prophetically exactly what we had just decided as a staff team – to bring the curtain down on the old way of being church, and to bring the curtain up on a new way. The old way involved a few people doing everything at the front and everyone else sitting and listening. The new way involved everyone being at the front and everyone being released to be contributors, not consumers. I was so encouraged by this confirmation of what he had heard during the day that I forwarded the email to the whole staff team. They too shared in the joy of hearing the Father's voice once again.

That night, Drew went to an MSC in Croxley Green called Open Door. He remembers looking around at all the people there and thinking, 'Oh my goodness, they have no idea what's about to happen.' Within a few years this one MSC would have grown into two more, doing great things for the Lord in mission.

On Wednesday we met for an emergency meeting of the PCC and informed everyone what we were about to do. There were wise and helpful questions about details but no one contested the big picture. The unity in the staff was obvious too. We were all systems go for a September departure from the building.

The rest of the week was spent putting together registration packs for the Sunday services. Drew met with all the existing MSC leaders before Sunday to tell them what we were all about to do. I prepared sermons for all four services. On Sunday I preached a message throughout the day entitled 'Preparing for Change'. I focused on the miracle of multiplication in Matthew 14, and particularly on the four actions of Jesus: he took, blessed, broke and distributed the bread. I pointed out that the bread is symbolic of Christ's body in the stories of the Last Supper. I also reminded the congregation that the church is the body of Christ, and I quoted St Augustine's memorable words: 'You are the Body of Christ. In you and through you the work of the incarnation must go forward. You are to be taken. You are to be blessed, broken and distributed, that you may be the means of grace and vehicles of eternal love.' Finally, I stressed the truth that the miracle of multiplication only occurred once the bread had been broken and I decreed over the church that our imminent fragmentation into 'vehicles of eternal love' was not going to lead to division but to multiplication. You could feel the excitement throughout the day. Above all you could sense the cloud of the presence of God's glory. His favour was clearly on what we were doing, and while a few were concerned about losing the cruise ship, the majority were very excited about launching the lifeboats. Faith was rising, and we were about to embark on a great adventure together.

God's perfect timing

From that time on, every week, people started to register for the MSCs to be formed by September. Each week, our Sunday bulletin sheets would include the number that had registered so far. This gave encouragement to the late adopters that everyone else was getting on board – and so should they.

It was also during that time that the builders asked for the refurbishment to be put back to January 2005. At first we were alarmed by this. We had built up a considerable amount of momentum in the weeks after the staff away-day in June. Would we lose that momentum now that we were going to delay the Exodus by four months? In the end we saw the sovereign hand of God in this, as in everything else we have witnessed over the years. The extra four months gave precious time for more thorough preparation.

This was important for several reasons. First of all, it gave Drew and his team time to identify leaders and place church members in the right MSCs. Drew, Judith, David and Jenny took a few more trips to Sheffield and back (a round trip of about six to seven hours) to consult with Bob and Mary Hopkins. During those long car journeys, they would read out the names of every person that had registered and discern which MSC they would offer to that church member. This was a long and painstaking process (much aided by David Rosser's capacity to read in the car without feeling carsick) and was followed by a personal signed letter from Drew to each person inviting them to join a particular MSC. These car journeys were clearly productive because when almost a thousand letters went out, by and large our people were very happy with the MSC that had been offered to them.

The second thing this did was allow us time to train the new leaders. In truth, we did not have any kind of leadership training course at the time. That was to come much later. But we did set aside a Saturday in September when we could gather all the existing and new MSC leaders at the church centre for a day of equipping. Bob and Mary Hopkins, along with a team from St Thomas' Crookes in Sheffield, came down and led the day. That day was a great blessing. And it was memorable for another reason. It was the same day that I was giving my address in London in the theological exchange with the Archbishop of Canterbury. Drew therefore showed a film of me giving words of encouragement to the MSC leaders while I was giving my presentation in London. This is what I said on the DVD: 'The development of mid-size communities is the top priority for the coming season at St Andrew's Church. It is an absolutely vital key to the fulfilment of our vision – to minister the Father's love and make disciples of Jesus in Chorleywood and beyond. If we can form successfully into MSCs we will be well on our way towards establishing a mission-shaped church that can truly move in revival rather than just survival mode. I want to endorse 100 per cent the strategy to establish MSCs and I want to urge all of us to step out of the boat and get involved in leading and serving an MSC on the frontiers of mission. This is the way forward for the twenty-first-century church. MSCs are the nets in which we are going to catch the fish – and in great numbers . . .'

The third thing the extra time gave us was the chance of having a trial run with our MSCs. Having done the amazing work of getting almost everyone into MSCs, Drew and his team chose a Sunday in October, November and December when all the MSCs could practise what would become normative in the New Year.

These three meetings were invaluable. They allowed us
to iron out a few leadership teething issues, and they
also gave people a taste of the goodness of being set free
to exercise their considerable gifts in mission. On the
three Sundays when we met back at St Andrew's, we
asked people to share their stories of what the Holy
Spirit had been doing in and through them on the
Sundays out in the MSCs. Their faces were radiant as
they shared. Later, I remember listening to the recording
of one of those testimony times in my car on a long journey. It was electric.

The final thing that this bonus time gave us was the
opportunity to ready the church through preaching the
Word. It is really hard to overemphasise the value of the
pulpit in the preparation for major change. This responsibility falls on the senior leader. He is the one who
needs to sound a clear note on the trumpet so that all the
people can get ready for battle. In the weeks from
September to December I embarked on a long series on
Matthew 14:22–32 entitled 'Walking on Water'. The titles
for these messages were:

- Setting Sail for a New Horizon
- Enduring the Winds of Change
- Facing our Fear of the New
- Discerning the Call to Step Out
- Moving out of our Comfort Zones
- Keeping our Eyes Fixed on Jesus
- Enjoying the Rewards of Faith

During these weeks of preaching, I spoke about 'the psy-
chology of transition'; that is, the different emotions that
we go through during times of situational change. Using
William Bridges' terminology, I spoke to the congregation about the three stages we were about to enter, and

the feelings likely to be experienced in each. Bridges calls these 'endings', 'the neutral zone', and 'beginnings':

Endings	Dealing with Loss	Anxiety, Blame, Fear, Shock
Neutral Zone	Transitional Period	Anxiety, Confusion, Uncertainty
Beginnings	Setting New Goals	Integration, Reinventing Yourself

Through preaching, we prepared ourselves for the ending of the current season in our building, the neutral zone while we were out of the building, and the new beginnings when we had the building back. I warned people that this experience would change us for ever. Above all, I emphasised the point that we don't go to church. We are the church.

The *kairos* moment arrives

Christmas arrived and we all prepared to celebrate the season in style. The clock was ticking. By now pretty well every man, woman and child associated with our church had signed up and been allocated an MSC. We also had about one hundred brand new leaders whom we commissioned in a very memorable service. I will never forget looking at these ordinary men and women endowed with an extraordinary calling and purpose. They all stood on the stage at the front of the church. All

I could think of was Steve's vision, received on 7 June, of a crowded stage. The drab grey had disappeared. It seemed as if the whole sanctuary was filled with colour. God's people were about to be released in mission. The curtain had come up on a new day.

And so we prepared for the first Sunday in January 2005. Somehow, in the whole process of decreeing this new adventure, the church had already started to grow dramatically. We reckoned at the start of 2004 that our congregation numbered about six hundred. By the time we were ready to leave the building at the end of December we had 976 men, women and children allocated to MSCs. Only a tiny handful of the existing congregation said no to the invitation to be sent out in mission. The vast majority said a resounding yes, most of them with a sense of faith and excitement, a few with trepidation and the occasional lament. All of us prepared for the divinely orchestrated moment of departure. As the day grew nearer, we all prepared for God's *kairos* moment.

It is well known that in the New Testament there are two words for 'time'. The first is *chronos*, from which we get our word 'chronology'. This is ordinary, everyday, continuous clock time. The second word is *kairos*. This is not ordinary time but extraordinary time. *Kairos* is a moment of opportunity that opens up and which has to be seized. In ancient Greek, the word was used of a small aperture through which an arrow had to pass in order to hit its target. *Kairos* time is unique time. If *chronos* is quantitative, *kairos* is qualitative.

What I learned through the whole process of preparing for the first Sunday in January was the importance of discerning *kairos* moments of opportunity. Most leaders are taught how to manage time. In other words, they are trained in *chronology*, in managing the process of clock time, sequencing priorities, etc. What they are not trained in is the far more intuitive art of what we might call *kairology*. This is the special ability to see when a unique aperture of opportunity has appeared and to seize the moment with both hands.

Moses excelled in this rare gift. There is so much about time in his life. Moses was certainly familiar with *chronos*. There are three main parts to his 120-year life. The first forty years were spent in Egypt (the place of education), the second in the desert of Midian (the place of preparation) and the third in the wilderness leading the people of Israel towards the Promised Land (the place of application). In all three of these parts of his life Moses came to know an awful lot about *chronos*, the passing of ordinary time. There must have been many occasions when Moses cried out, 'How long, Lord?'

However, Moses also learned the art of seizing the *kairos* moment. Having encountered the Lord at the burning bush, Moses goes back to Egypt and tells his own people what God has commanded. They are at this stage convinced. Moses then goes to confront Pharaoh, who laughs in his face and puts the squeeze on the Hebrew people – forcing them to make even more bricks, but now without recourse to straw.

At this point it would have been easy for Moses to give up. Pharaoh had laughed in his face and his own people had moaned to him that their situation was even worse. However, it is precisely at this point that the aperture of opportunity opens up. Just when it seemed as if things couldn't get worse, we read the following in Exodus 6:1 (NKJV): 'Then the Lord said to Moses, "Now you shall see what I will do to Pharaoh. For with a strong hand he will let them go, and with a strong hand he will drive them out of his land."' Notice the little word 'now'. This word is *attah* in

Hebrew and means 'right now, straightaway, at this very moment'.

Moses is at a *kairos* moment, and far from running from it in fear he seizes it by faith. This is the time for the plagues to be released. One after another, in the space of several weeks, at strategic moments designated precisely by the Lord, Moses goes to confront Pharaoh and release the signs of God's power and judgement. Only after the tenth plague – the death of the first-born sons of Egypt – does Pharaoh relent and release the Hebrew people. As soon as he did so, the Hebrew people also seized the moment. Under Moses' leadership, they too passed through the aperture of opportunity. As we read in Exodus 12:37 (NLT), 'That night the people of Israel left Rameses and started for Succoth. There were about 600,000 men, plus all the women and children. And they were all travelling on foot.' The writer goes on to add in verses 40–42: 'The people of Israel had lived in Egypt for 430 years. In fact, it was on the last day of the 430th year that all the LORD's forces left the land. This night had been reserved by the LORD to bring his people out from the land of Egypt, so this same night now belongs to him. It must be celebrated every year, from generation to generation, to remember the LORD's deliverance.' After 430 years of *chronos*, there is a *kairos* time for God's people. Under Moses' expert and anointed leadership, preparation meets opportunity and all the people leave.

From Moses' example we can see that timing is critical to courageous leadership. Jesus also modelled this: after thirty years of preparation (the 'hidden years', as they are sometimes called), he left his home town and travelled to the River Jordan, where he was baptised. He spent forty days in the desert before coming out and announcing, 'At last the time has come' (the word is *kairos* in Mark 1:15).

Spiritual leadership often involves a slow process of influencing people over months and even years. At the same time, this slow process includes sudden moments of opportunity that need to be seized courageously if there is to be acceleration and advancement. So how do you know when such moments are before you?

Knowing a *kairos* moment is mainly the product of experience. The longer you spend in leadership, the better you get at sensing when you have to seize the day. Perhaps in this respect it is no accident that the writer of Exodus tells us in Exodus 7:7 (NLT), 'Moses was eighty years old, and Aaron was eighty-three at the time they made their demands to Pharaoh.' They had experience on their side!

One of the ten plagues that Moses witnesses is the plague of locusts (Exodus 10:1–20). At a designated moment, Moses raises his staff and God causes an east wind to begin to blow. This wind brings the worst swarm of locusts ever seen in Egypt.

Locusts are important because they teach us about timing. The wings of a locust are thin and small. They jump in an attempt to fly, leaping into the air. But until the wind comes they merely practise (and often injure themselves). When the wind comes, however, they can jump up to one hundred times as far into the air and glide for hundreds of miles. So the key for the locust is to wait for the sound of the rustling of the wind in the trees. Then they know 'IT'S TIME TO JUMP' and they all jump together.

Locusts know when the wind has arrived and it's time to fly. Effective leaders are people who are proficient at knowing when the wind of God's Spirit is blowing in a new direction and who influence their people to jump together. In jumping together, God's people are empowered to jump further than they ever could on their own.

Spiritual leaders are therefore like the sons of Issachar, who understood the times (1 Chronicles 12:32).

On the first Sunday in January 2005, God's people responded at the critical moment and there was a great exodus. God had been speaking to me all year, 'Let my people go!' On 2 January – the day after New Year's Day – the people of God left the church and became the church. All I can remember of that day is waking up thinking, 'Oh my Lord, what have I done? I have just given away the whole church!' And a voice immediately responded, 'Precisely.'

It is a day I will never forget.

It turned out in the end to be one of the happiest days of my life.

5

BREAKING OUT OF THE BOX

Andrew Williams

The Lord had shown us that if our MSCs were to be authentic they had to be vision-led; this was grass-roots and bottom-up as a strategy. This meant that new leaders had to come to us. Having been asked the question, 'What is the Lord saying to you?' almost all of our fledgling MSCs began with a slightly nervous member of our church family making a telephone call or writing an email or coming up to us in the street and saying, 'I think the Lord has been speaking to me.' And as they spoke of what the Lord had laid upon their hearts we glimpsed the beginnings of a new adventure in mission. We were also able to link them with other church members who had come to us and spoken in similar terms. All over Chorleywood and the surrounding area there were prayer meetings breaking out as new leadership teams were getting together for the first time and seeking the Lord for their MSC.

To be perfectly honest, I found all this to be a very risky and nerve-racking way of going about things, but it was clearly the way the Lord wanted the job done. I don't have too many pretensions (the last few years have been extraordinarily refining), but at that time I did feel a very special empathy with Noah. Not unlike Noah, here were the Lord's very clear instructions and here was a very large pile of wood and nails with which to build. We were feverishly hammering away as fast as we could, but the nagging doubt in my mind was, 'Will there be enough wood to build these arks?' Every day more and more people were signing up to be part of an MSC. We jumped from six hundred to seven hundred and then miraculously to 976 men, women and children. Somehow the Holy Spirit kindled a spirit of adventure in many of our people and a spirit of faithfulness in many others. For us to be able to decant these rescuers into lifeboats we needed coxswains. The Lord was faithful. As the numbers of willing crew increased so did the leaders, generally in twos as it happened.

Around these leaders' visions for mission we were able to direct our people and slowly and surely the lifeboats were built and filled. This meant that the MSC map was more diverse and more creative than we could have conceived or planned. We had MSCs for the youth, for the elderly, for the deaf community, for many different neighbourhoods and communities. We had MSCs planning to meet in Starbucks, community halls, school halls, Scout huts, in the midst of car boot sales and even in Café Nero. Given that the Roman Emperor Nero had ruthlessly persecuted Christians, the historical irony of this was curious. Nero's also agreed to serve the MSC coffee at a discount price, which was insufficient recompense for Caesar's bad attitude but a nice touch nevertheless.

I recall an early evening meeting with some of our new MSC leaders. We had shared a meal together and told stories of all that the Lord was doing. When I came to leave, every new leader around that table approached me privately and told me that they had been carrying the vision for what they were now a part of for many years – some of them for as long as twenty years. It took me over an hour to leave. The gold reserve was far bigger than even I had anticipated. I drove home that night humbled by their faith and patience. I was also struck with the density of population all around us; street after street, tower block after tower block, thousands upon thousands of people – all of them children of the King and the largest number of them living as spiritual paupers. It struck me that if this were to change, we would need every ounce of vision and compassion that the Lord had ever invested in every one of his people. To reach such a multitude would take everything we had.

Riding the range

Each Sunday morning the staff would gather in the chapel for prayer and then head out to visit the MSCs. Borrowing from St Thomas', we called this 'riding the range'. For me this meant a plethora of driving directions stuck to the dashboard of my car. It also meant quite a large amount of time spent in various lay-bys, wrestling with an AA road map, and the vain hope that if I was still lost by nightfall, maybe I could identify the pole star. When I eventually arrived, the brief was to encourage, maybe even to say a few words, but not to interfere in the meeting. I think that some of our MSC leaders thought that we were like Ofsted inspectors. This was far from the truth. We were all learning together. Indeed, if they had seen me in the lay-by they would have known not to be unduly concerned.

To be perfectly honest, after years of being in church on a Sunday morning it was nice to get out for a bit. What was immediately evident to me was that while we were all in church doing our thing the rest of the world was out there in the community getting on with their own lives, and very happily too, thank you very much. It would be nice to say that the rest of the world missed us or that our not being around on a Sunday made a bit more space in the supermarket aisles, but that would not be true.

The immediate question was, would anybody notice the people of God now that we had come out of hiding? When I had first cast the strategy someone had said to me, 'What difference will it make if a few Christians are meeting in a school hall somewhere? Who would know that they were there?' Actually, that was a fair point, but that was until we got out of the church building and realised that we were no longer wearing our invisibility cloak. Just by being there, our people were impacting communities in completely unexpected ways. MSCs that were meeting in school halls suddenly found that they were receiving invitations to take assemblies or to run after-school clubs. One of our MSCs met in a school hall where the roof was partially made of glass. Sunday by Sunday there were some lads carrying out their community service orders by repairing it. These young lads had a grandstand view as they looked down from on high and watched all that was going on below with the MSC. Very soon coffee and a supply of homemade sponge cake and cookies were being passed up to the rooftop. I cannot say that in this time one of those lads gave his life to Jesus. I know that the MSC would have loved that and they were certainly all praying for their rooftop visitors. I also know that these young guys (perhaps not everyone's favourite young people in the wider community) were surprised and touched by this unexpected demonstration of the Father's love through the actions of our people.

The MSC known as The Way was meeting in a community hall where every room was packed with activity groups on a Sunday morning. Parents would drop their kids off and after a while they would accept the offer of a cup of coffee from our MSC members. The hallway in this community centre was long and thin, with seating all the way down. The MSC were in a room at the end of the hall and would deliberately keep the door open. They could not help but notice that parents would deliberately choose to come and sit outside their open door so that they could listen in to what was going on. After a while they put a prayer box in the hallway with a simple invitation offering to pray in confidence. Sure enough the prayer box was used and this led to some interesting conversations and some wonderful answers to prayer.

Open Door MSC, meeting in a school hall, found that on a Sunday the school grounds were also being used for a local children's football club. They seized the opportunity and served refreshments to the parents and younger brothers and sisters, and before long these children were joining the MSC children's work that was going on inside the hall. There was a wonderful naturalness in all of this. From another MSC one member commented, 'I am struck by the authenticity of what we are doing. You can't help but talk about what God is doing in the MSC at work on Monday morning.' The Ark reported, 'We had about eleven visitors to our breakfast and guest meeting. We feel that our presence is making an impact in the community.' Another leader told us, 'God is teaching us how to be an MSC. We make mistakes but we are growing step by step into what God wants us to be. We are doing some gardening to bless the community. We have had four houses accept our offer. Another household say that they want to come to our gathering next Sunday. We are also having a barbecue – after we've done the gardening – and a local family has accepted our invitation to come to that.' Touching community even further afield, The Pump House MSC stocked a freshwater pond with fish at an orphanage in Uganda.

St Andrew's had long been blessed by a very gifted and dedicated signing team for the deaf. Building on all that they had done, we were thrilled to see an MSC formed whose mandate was to reach out to the deaf community. The name of the MSC is Hand in Hand, and in the early days one of the leaders wrote to me with this testimony:

> I can honestly say that leading an MSC for the last eight months has been the hardest and most challenging thing I have ever done – parenthood aside. In running the MSC I have discovered a lot of things about myself. Some I knew already and others are fresh revelations. I am not a brilliant administrator, neither am I a preacher. I don't think I am a worship leader or a kids' ministry leader, but I have had to do all these things and more at some stage or another and I discovered that I can passably lead prayers, make OK coffee, improvise a kids' session, preach if necessary, impart difficult decisions. Above all – boy, can I flap! But our God is a gracious God and I know that I am not alone and that he uses my weaknesses.

All of our leaders from all of our MSCs could relate to these sentiments. What makes this testimony special is that the lady writing is deaf.

These were still early days and our pioneer MSCs were finding the lie of the land, but in these small beginnings we could see that the Kingdom of God was breaking out in our midst.

The magnificent 77

Our church family were now thriving in their gifting. In January 2004 (before the exodus) just five people had preached at St Andrew's during the course of the month. A year on, in dispersed MSCs, 77 people preached in the month of January. And they did a fantastic job. Using Rick Warren's *The Purpose Driven Life*, Mark recast its message through Paul's letter to the Ephesians. This material was then sent out to the MSC leaders a month or so in advance. Suddenly the Word of God as it related to community, service, purpose and mission took on a whole new sharpness. We would encourage our leaders not to be bound by teaching notes as a script but to read the material and teach on what excited their hearts. Being out on the field brought such life to God's Word and it also brought life to God's people. It may have been raw on occasion but it was always passionate. Everybody knew that this was, say, Nick's first time to speak. Everybody was rooting for him, and you could have heard a pin drop as Nick, using the theological framework of the notes, shared. What is more, transformation was taking place in the hearts of our people as the message was given.

Before we abandoned the cruise ship, I had spent quite some time with a church member. Her sense of self-worth was very low. In order to hear what she was saying I had to sit on the edge of my seat, straining to hear what was left of her spirit. It was as if all that she had suffered had robbed her of her voice. My heart bled for her. You can imagine my total and utter astonishment to walk into the back of her MSC and find her at a keyboard, playing and singing as she led the community in worship. There was something about belonging

and purpose that was very healing, and this was only
the beginning.

One morning I was visiting our MSC out in Ruislip.
This mission community had immediately developed
something of an international flavour, with members
coming from all over the world. As I came into the hall
there were about thirty people all laughing and talking
together. I was immediately passed a cup of good coffee
and a piece of South African cake. I also noticed that
amidst the aroma of coffee and conversation there were
some new faces. Before I could get to them I was being
enthusiastically introduced: 'This is my friend – they
live in my street.' Then the group was called to an informal sort of order, after which newcomers were welcomed and people shared how the Lord had met with
them in the week. There was such warmth and affection
in the way that they listened to each other. There was a
little bit of teaching and then we were asked to break
into small groups where we listened to each other and
applied what we had been taught. Two new members
from Norway sang a worship song that they had written
in the previous week. Everyone naturally responded
with applause. The musicians looked a little bashful
with all the attention, but the song was beautiful and
everybody said so. Another member stood up and
explained that they were going to organise a team to
help out at the local community hall fair. The plan was
for the MSC members to serve at the fair by volunteer-
ing to do the clearing up and packing away. A lot of
hands went up – including those of some of the newcomers. There was such a transparent goodness in what
was going on around me. How could you be against
this? The meeting closed with a short time of prayer and
the boldness of my own private petition surprised me:
'Lord, I will fight for this.'

Fourth Sunday pilgrimage

As well as all this activity going on Sunday by Sunday, an important part of the strategy was to get everyone together for a big fourth Sunday Celebration. This was a huge piece of church to orchestrate. We found the biggest school hall we could find and our sound engineer Paul Davison worked around the clock to put together a PA system that would enable us all to hear. We brought in audio-visual equipment, flowers, musicians, singers, intercessors and a welcome team that would have done Wembley Arena proud. We emptied St Andrew's vault of all the best family silver so that we could all come together in Holy Communion. Every department in the church went into overdrive but it was worth it. Every MSC shut up shop and all our people filled the hall. Suddenly what had once been just an every-Sunday habit became something very special, almost like a pilgrimage.

This was also a great opportunity to share good news. One of our children's pastors, Dave Hill, and I borrowed a DVD camera and spent two weekends racing around the neighbourhood filming what was going on in all the different MSCs. Dave is a natural in front of the camera but I want to pay tribute to his masterful inventiveness in the art of film-making, which included balancing one of our star interns, Zach, on a shopping trolley and pushing him down a hill towards a community hall at high speed. We edited the footage into a four-minute film. The overall effect was astonishing and we showed this film to the whole church at a fourth Sunday service. It was invaluable for the whole church family to be able to see with their own eyes the creativity and breadth in what we were all doing.

Back on the home front

Unwittingly I had put my wife slap bang on the front line. Elena had been willing to lead an MSC and with a very gifted and faithful leadership team she hired a local hall in Chorleywood; soon her MSC was booming. And that was my first big mistake. At that time we were attempting to put a ceiling on membership at seventy-two adult members. It had a nice ring about it: Jesus had the twelve and then of course sent out the seventy-two. Tucked just down the road from St Andrew's, Elena's MSC was a popular destination – and having already disappointed quite a few people who would have liked to be members, they began life with a complement of almost eighty people.

There were some very noble things that came out of this MSC (not least some strong and enduring friendships) and there were many people who worked incredibly hard to make it a success, but it was quite simply too big. I had sunk them before they got out of the harbour. Immediately attendance figures dropped off as the sheer mass of people militated against a sense of shared vision, ownership and belonging. There were one or two who were very trenchant in their criticism and it was difficult for the team to make headway under growing crossfire. This is a strategy that thrives on encouragement and withers pretty quickly where there is no grace.

At the same time Elena's mystery illness was creeping into our bedroom late at night and violently waking her with intense pain. We were becoming very familiar with the curious route through Watford to the General Hospital. If we had been collecting air miles we could have taken the girls to Disney World. We saw a number of doctors and specialists. Elena was screened, scanned and tested for everything under the sun and yet nobody was any the wiser. We had hoped that it might be possible to have a third child, but until whatever was causing her such pain was diagnosed, carrying a baby was simply out of the question.

Joshua calling

Although I was thrilled with all that the Lord was doing through the MSCs and their crews, I have to confess that at this point in our story, on the inside I was dying a little bit. It felt like all of my gifts were atrophying. I recall one morning just losing it in a lay-by, trying to work out which way round the M25 I was not headed. 'What are you doing, Lord? You know that I can't navigate my way out of a paper bag and yet here I am at the side of the road, again, lost and late – while everybody else is doing what I thought you called me to do. What are you trying to do, kill me?' There was an eerie silence which I took to be affirmative. There was a lot of dying to me in all of this. The role of associate vicar was not straightforward and required an excess of grace that the Lord was still in the process of refining in me.

Mark discerned that the leadership team needed a pick-me-up, so with Jim Sutton and a good friend and former colleague, Greg Downes, we took a trip to . . . Bracknell. Dr Stibbe is generous like that! There was a Willow Creek conference in town and Mark thought it would do us all good to get out of the heat and have some input from Bill Hybels and an impressive team of guest speakers.

The journey down was memorable. Greg consumed two cans of Red Bull before breakfast and was taking the rest of us, at the speed of light, through a theological discourse on Pauline hermeneutics, and all before 8 o'clock in the morning. We had a good breakfast at a motorway service station (we made Greg sit at another table) and I shared with the team that we had grown within our first month by about fifty new members. Some of these had moved to the area (from as far away as South Africa) but the majority were neighbours and friends who had vowed never to set foot across the threshold of a church but were enjoying the community that had turned up on their doorstep. One of these was a lovely lady called Joyce who had made such a vow, which her friend and neighbour Barbara, a long-time member at St Andrew's, had been unable to persuade her to break. Barbara's MSC, meeting in a primary school in north Watford, was, however, an invitation that Joyce did feel able to accept and very shortly afterwards she accepted Jesus as her Saviour. So there was much rejoicing over sausage, eggs and fried tomatoes – except for Greg, who was on the Atkins diet and passed on the tomatoes, ate Jim's sausage and then put away a few rounds of toast.

The conference was great. The speakers were outstanding, and so much of what we were hearing was affirming of what we were doing. But the Lord saved the best until last. If you have never heard T.D. Jakes preach you have missed out. The man is a mountain for God! Taking Moses as his theme, he spoke about leadership in a way that I had not heard before. My batteries were recharging with all this godly wisdom. But then the man-mountain turned his attention to Joshua, and this is what he said:

> Joshua was a gifted leader in his own right, hands-on with the people, a strategist, a firefighter, someone who exercised compassion but who was not afraid of confrontation; someone who exercised his leadership ministry within the complexities of Moses' leadership and

ministry. Joshua was a man who was totally loyal to Moses and who would not split the flock.

There are times when the Father speaks so clearly to you as a son that it just breaks you. This was one of those times. My notes were covered with cerulean blue blots where my tears were hitting the page so hard that they made the ink blow out in little concentric circles. My Heavenly Father was saying, 'Son, this is who you are – you are a Joshua.' This was the call that everything else needed to die to. Whatever my fleshly ambition to be 'the Leader', here in this simple statement was my bona fide calling in God for as long as this season lasted. There was suddenly such a breathtaking clarity in who I was and what I was supposed to do. All of the hundreds of meetings with MSC leaders, all the confrontations, the sense of having been equipped with a fireman's hard hat as well as the helmet of salvation, all the strategising, all the communicating and casting vision and fanning the embers of calling in so many others, all made sense. This was not death – this was life.

Haven

About a month after we had moved out of the building, two of our church members, Janet Hosier and Elaine Dean, put a brown envelope into my hand with a proposal for an MSC. I am ashamed to admit that in all the busyness, this envelope stayed on my desk for a short while before I opened it. Judith spotted this and put it at the top of the pile. The envelope contained some very exciting news. Many years before, Janet had felt led by the Lord to open her home to the homeless for an evening meal. This became so popular that the Lord led them to buy a bus that was parked on some land in Watford, where many people were given a good meal and shown the Father's love. From the bus developed night shelters and a day centre, and today this ministry, the Watford New Hope Trust, has grown to be the largest supplier of services to the homeless in the county.

Janet had long sensed the Lord's calling to build a place of Christian nurture and discipleship at the centre. Many of their clients had expressed an interest in the Christian faith but the prospect of turning up at church was a bridge too far. Janet and her colleague Elaine had a wonderful proposal – could we build an MSC within Watford New Hope Trust? The answer was of course yes, and this MSC was given the name 'Haven'.

As time went on, Haven MSC multiplied into two MSCs serving the homeless in Watford. We would see Haven MSC members on the hospitality team at St Andrew's, serving coffee, welcoming at the door and joining the worship band with improvised jazz piano solos. Haven MSC members would go on to give testimony to their new-found faith in Jesus Christ as they were baptised at the church centre. Janet would write and tell me, 'The baptism was wonderful, he looked so happy, said he felt so clean inside and the feeling he had in the pool was greater than any alcohol- or drug-induced high.' All of this was to come, but in 2005 Haven sounded a prophetic call to the church to move out in this strategy with increased mercy. I count it a very great privilege to be able to work with Haven MSC. I always understood this addition to our portfolio of mission and mercy to be a sign of the Lord's affirmation and trust in our labours.

'Your left eye is a dog's dinner'

That summer, Mark, David, Jenny and I were invited to Norway to speak at a Christian conference – Oasis – on building a mission-shaped church. Elena and Alie came along too. We spoke over two days. None of us felt like experts but it was good to share some of the goodness of what the Lord was doing in our midst. The first day went really well. Norwegians are not typically excessive in demonstrating their emotions, but in their own Nordic way they were wildly enthusiastic: there was moderate clapping and nobody fell asleep. The second day, however, was not nearly as much fun. The DVD presentation did not work and we did not communicate very clearly; it was like walking through treacle. My part was to speak on spiritual warfare and the essential place of prayer in this strategy. Although we were all feeling that the session had not gone as well as we had hoped, when we offered to pray for the delegates at the end of the seminar, they nearly all came forward and we had a powerful time of ministry.

That night the St Andrew's team all went out for supper. We ate in a strange little restaurant that served sushi and cold beer. We ate sushi (cautiously), we drank cold beer (modestly) and we retired to bed (fairly early); we know how to have a good time! At about midnight I woke up with terrible pains in my stomach; so severe that I had to run very, very quickly to the bathroom. I was also running with sweat and (being a man and never having given birth to a child) I wondered if this was the moment that I was actually going to die. Elena was in the bedroom and she says that she heard me cry out. I don't remember that. If I did, I expect it was a manly sort of low cry and not a feverish girly squeal as has since been unfairly suggested.

I don't remember what happened after that. I do remember Elena's voice saying, 'Drew, Drew!' And I do recall just seeing white – nothing but bright white light and the feeling of warmth. The bright white light turned out to be the white stone tiles that I was lying on. The warmth was my blood which was now soaking into Norwegian grouting at about one square foot per second.

I said, with as much dignity as could be mustered by someone who had just dived head first off the toilet onto a tiled concrete floor with his backside in the air, 'I think I know what is going on here.' Elena said that she had a pretty good idea too and she helped me up. It was then that I caught sight of myself in the bathroom mirror. You could see the inside of my head! There was blood spurting out all over the wall and the bathroom now looked like an Alfred Hitchcock set.

At the same time, the other issues that had taken me to the bathroom so promptly were still issuing. I decided to take faith action. Sitting in my own blood, I closed my eyes – well, I closed my one good eye – and I prayed, 'Father, I need to get to hospital to get stitched up. I can't do stitches, profuse bleeding, vomiting and diarrhoea.' I thought maybe if I offered the Lord a choice of which ailment he might prefer to heal this might assist. So I prayed, 'Lord, there is a Norwegian smorgasbord of infirmities here – take your pick – all healing gratefully received. Amen.' You will understand that it had to be a quick prayer. From that moment the nausea and the other debilitating condition just stopped.

Elena and I got a taxi and headed off to the hospital. Very soon a Norwegian nurse and a doctor (who curiously enough was trained in Hull and had an intriguing Norwegian/Yorkshire accent) were busy sewing me back together. I can't imagine how painful it must be to be sewn up without an analgesic, because the twelve or so injections they put into the open wound to anaesthetise the pain were agonising. There were hands moving all over my face with syringes and cloths and needle and thread. Elena was holding my hand and I think I almost crushed her fingers. Then the nurse broke the news that my mum and dad were in the waiting room. I thought, my goodness, this is it, they have flown in my parents: I must be dying. It turned out that 'Mum and Dad' were David and Jenny, who had followed my trail of blood from the hotel to the hospital. We were pleased to see them and of course they were praying for me. Actually my Visa card was declined, so they also ended up paying for me. The Norwegian doctor with the Yorkshire accent said, 'Ee, lad, we have sewn up thy face – but your left eye is a dog's dinner. We've done t'best we can!'

The walk back from the hospital to the hotel was memorable. Elena, David and Jenny were propping me up as we made our way through a little park. It was a very warm night and it must have been about three in the morning. We could not stop laughing, with me saying, 'Stop! It hurts when I laugh,' which of course encouraged them all the more. At the time I felt that if this incident was some form of spiritual attack it was vastly disproportionate to the very small contribution that we made to the Oasis conference that year. Today, as I recall these events, the MSC experience at St Andrew's has become a helpful resource for a growing number of Norwegian churches who are transitioning to a gathered and dispersed model. I think if anybody had told us that on this particular night, we would have laughed even louder.

No going back

Back at St Andrew's great things were happening. Before we had begun this adventure I could not get small groups started for love nor money. I had not given small groups a tremendous amount of attention in this period of the refurbishment, because all our efforts were being poured into keeping the MSCs fit and well. I did a quick audit at the end of this season and was overwhelmed to find that we had grown twenty-two new small groups without even trying. Because busy people had been given the opportunity to get to know one another properly, now they were willing to invest some additional time in a midweek small group. Our MSC leaders were thriving in their gifting. Leadership teams and MSCs were growing. Overall our church membership had grown by about 150 new people in this season. It was then that we heard the rumour that many of the MSCs had been praying that the refurbishment works would be delayed so that they could continue to meet. The refurbishment works had in fact gone well. Jim Sutton, our church manager, had masterminded the building project with a committed team – but it had now come to our attention that when the new church doors opened, we would not physically fit inside the building.

This was a time of some quite high tension across the church. Rudyard Kipling famously commended in his poem 'If', 'If you can keep your head when all about you are losing theirs and blaming it on you . . . Yours is the Earth and everything that's in it, and, which is more, you'll be a man, my son.' For me, this poem will always be synonymous with this season and Kipling's commendation exemplified in Mark's leadership.

We encouraged an extensive time of listening, to each other and to the Lord. And then, one summer's night, me still nursing a dog's dinner of a left eye, we assembled all the MSC leaders in a local hall. We put an open mike at the front and one by one the MSC leaders gave a summary of their members' feelings and their sense of the Lord's onward call. With the exception of one MSC, they all said the same thing: 'We have only just got started in this adventure – there is no going back.' It was a warm evening and I went outside for a breath of fresh air. I looked back at the building where all our MSC leaders were praising God and praying for each other. For an instant, I may just have glimpsed angels, in great number, on the roof of the building, all rejoicing.

6

THE GENIUS OF 'AND'

Mark Stibbe

On the first Sunday in January 2005 I woke up with a profound feeling of loss and insecurity. I had just let go of the whole congregation and released them into MSCs. The church building across the car park from the vicarage was now about to be turned into a building site. I remember experiencing a cold sweat as I realised how disoriented I felt. What would I do with no church building to go to, no people to lead, and no sermons to preach? I was a vicar, after all. We may not get paid very much, but we are employed to meet certain traditional expectations. What would I do now that these could not be fulfilled?

The problem I was dealing with had to do with my identity. I had spent a good number of years teaching on the issue of our personal identity as adopted sons and daughters of the World's Greatest Dad. My life message was (and is) about our security being in our position, not in our performance, that we are sons and daughters, not slaves. What I hadn't appreciated was the degree to which I was still bound by a need to do something in order to earn the Father's love and other people's approval. On 2 January 2005, the Holy Spirit started dealing with this issue, peeling away another layer of the seemingly limitless onion of my soul. In the process my identity began to be separated from my ministry and I kept repeating to myself, 'I am, therefore I do, not I do, therefore I am.'

By the end of that first day out of the building, I was beginning to ask how on earth I could have been so blind for so long. Having been 'riding the range' to several brand new MSCs in the morning, I realised that this is what 'church' is all about – not people coming to a building to hear me, but rather a dynamic movement of people sent out with permission for mission and the opportunity to use their considerable gifts. On that momentous day I realised why the Father had been saying for a year, 'Let my people go that they may worship me in the desert.' For far too long I had been part of a system that encouraged people simply to sit passively in a provider–client, consumer culture. Now the Holy Spirit had removed the restraints and suddenly there was growth – growth spiritually and growth numerically. I recall the unbridled joy I felt as I sat and watched hundreds of other people using their gifts of leadership and communication, instead of having them sit and watch me use mine. It felt like the beginning of a new Reformation – of the priesthood of all believers in practice, not just in theory. We had started an exodus out of an old, oppressive system. The Promised Land of a new freedom lay ahead of us all. I couldn't wait!

There isn't a manual

In the nine months we spent out of the building, meeting three Sundays in MSCs and one Sunday in a big concert hall, I was constantly thinking about what lay ahead of us. For most of this time the church building was being slowly transformed into a brand new, multi-functional resource centre for our twenty-first-century mission. I knew from the start it was going to be an outstanding new facility, thanks to the great team that had worked so hard under Jim Sutton's diligent leadership in the planning stages. After the first Sunday out of the building, a thought began to cross my mind: 'We are spending nearly one million pounds on this facility. What do we do when it is finished in September?' Night and day I was going to the Father and praying, 'Please show me what we do when we get the building back.' Before we left the building I had thought, 'They won't want to leave.' Now that we had left I was thinking, 'They won't want to come back.' So I nagged God – what do I do, Lord?

The Bible calls this nagging 'enquiring of the Lord'. Some of the godly leaders of the Old Testament used to do this. Perhaps my favourite of all is King Jehoshaphat. He always sought the Lord for revelation. In 2 Chronicles 20:3 we read that 'Jehoshaphat resolved to enquire of the LORD'. I love that!

King Solomon was another leader who sought revelation for leadership decisions. We read in 2 Chronicles 1:7 that 'God appeared to Solomon and said to him, "Ask for whatever you want me to give you."' I wonder what you would have asked for. This is what Solomon replies in 2 Chronicles 1:8–10, and it is perhaps the reason for his great reputation for prudence:

> *'You have shown great kindness to David my father and have made me king in his place. Now, LORD God, let your promise to my father David be confirmed, for you have made me king over a people who are as numerous as the dust of the earth. Give me wisdom and knowledge, that I may lead this people, for who is able to govern this great people of yours?'*

I recall hearing my friend Ken Gott say something deceptively simple in Toronto in 1995. He said, 'Spiritual leadership is letting the Holy Spirit lead.' This was the challenge I was faced with – letting the Holy Spirit lead. As soon as we left the building, I asked daily for wisdom and knowledge from heaven. I sought the Lord for his plan for September, when we would have our building back. 'Where are you leading, Father?'

In the early days of 2005 I tried looking for a book on church growth that might give me the key to the next stage of our journey. I scanned the immediate horizon for a conference or at least a seminar that addressed the kinds of issues we were facing. I couldn't find anything. There simply wasn't anything. We were like people without a map. Over and over we kept repeating to one another the words of Joshua 3:4: 'Then you will know which way to go, since you have never been this way before.' It really was uncharted territory for us and we were every day totally reliant on the Holy Spirit to show us the way ahead.

Then one day I sensed the Father speak to me in these memorable words, which have since become something of a catchphrase for St Andrew's: 'There isn't a manual, but there is Immanuel.'

As soon as I heard this, I felt an extraordinary sense of inner serenity. My striving for guidance about the next stage ended: I began to rest. And in that place of rest, the Lord showed me his plan for when we got the building back, and he did so in a most unusual context through a most unusual source.

In the navy

Just at the point when I most needed to know 'what next?' I found myself in a lushly decorated lounge in a very smart hotel in the south of England. I was there on a speaking engagement. Having given my presentation I was now enjoying a cup of tea. A man about my age came and sat next to me. Mike was a navy man and wanted to know how things were going at St Andrew's. So I told him about the church refurbishment, the formation into MSCs and the extraordinary goodness of the Lord in the months that we had been out. He was attentive and clearly engaged by what he was hearing.

I then told him that our people had grown so significantly during the time away from the building that we were now in a bit of a quandary. What would we do in September when we were able to return to the building?

At this point I decided to ask Mike his view. His answer provided the key that unlocked the guidance I was desperate for.

Mike began by describing the changes that we had experienced as a church. He saw things very clearly and he saw them through naval lenses. He analysed the kind of church that we had been up to the time of Drew's arrival. 'In that stage,' he said, 'you were a battleship surrounded by a few escorts and your role was captain.'

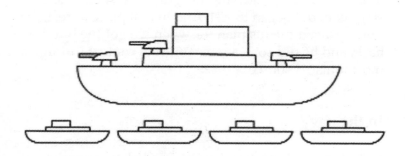

He identified the old St Andrew's as a battleship and our three church plants as escorts.

Mike then went on to explain that we had now changed into a task group. Instead of being a battleship surrounded by a few escorts, we were a flagship resourcing many task units. These task units were groups of smaller vessels with what Mike called 'a licence to hunt'. The flagship's role was one of support and communication. The task units' role was to patrol parts of the ocean that they were called to cover. In that process, the admiral on the flagship employed what is known as 'command by exception'. He effectively said to each task unit, 'I will not interfere with what you are doing except under two circumstances. One, you invite me to. Two, I see you going off course.' Mike said, 'Mark, are you aware that your church has turned from a battleship to a task group? Are you also aware that this church could grow beyond that at some future date, from being a task group to being a huge task force?'

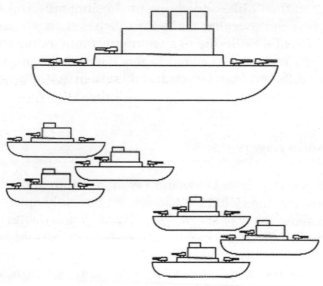

I remember the rising sense of excitement as Mike spoke. Here at last was the clarity I was seeking, provided by a naval officer over a cup of tea in a posh hotel. I couldn't have dreamed that scenario up in a million years!

Finally, I had to ask the 64 million dollar question. 'What would *you* do in my situation when the refurbishment is finished?' He replied, 'I would offer everyone a binary choice. Tell all of your church members that they can do one of two things. They can come back to the flagship and help resource the work of the task group, or they can stay out in their CTUs (Command Task Units) and act in liaison with the flagship. Either way, they need to know that their answer to this question is valid. If they decide to serve on the flagship, this does not mean that they are in any way less valuable than those who serve in the task units. Both those in the task units and those on the flagship are equally important.'

And then Mike added one final comment: 'And you, Mark, need to realise that your role has changed from a captain of a battleship to an admiral commanding a task group. You need to adjust to this new role because it is very different from before and there are big implications for your future.'

Another away-day

A few weeks later Drew and I went to a retreat centre to share together what we had sensed the Holy Spirit saying about the way ahead. We had not colluded with each other at all. The agreement was that we would write down what we sensed the Father was saying and would present the plans to one another and see how they dovetailed. We had booked the whole day in a log cabin, anticipating that it would take a long time to discover the plan and identify the practical implications.

In the end we were done by noon. The reason for this was that our two plans were almost identical. Drew recalls that we had both come up with about five points: four that were the same, and one that filled in the missing parts of the other's solution. It truly was a remarkable moment, one that highlights the very powerful synergy and unity that the Holy Spirit had formed in us as two leaders. By noon we were done and I suggested a long and well-earned lunch in a nearby pub in Northwood. We then took the plan to all the leaders of the church. Having fine-tuned it, we were ready to send out a paper to every member of the church, outlining the binary decision that they needed to make.

So what was the plan?

We decided to use what we have come to refer to as an 'orbital' model of church life. The phrase 'orbital leadership' came from John Paul Jackson on one of his visits to St Andrew's and it immediately grabbed us, not least because we are located just off the London orbital road, the M25. What we offered people was a choice: either come back into the centre and serve there, or stay in your MSC on a Sunday, but come into the centre on a rotational basis.

We made only two caveats.

First of all, every fourth Sunday we would continue to do what we had done during the nine months out. We would have celebrations in which I would communicate vision to the whole congregation. These services would be held morning and evening and would provide opportunities for strengthening the glue that held us together. We had really valued these expressions of 'gathered' church while we had been away from the building. We certainly didn't want to forgo that on our return. We believed then and believe now in the power of gathering everyone together, and we certainly value the goodness of monthly celebrations. No MSCs would meet that Sunday.

Secondly, Drew decided that whenever we had a month with a fifth Sunday, we would designate it a Rest and Resource Sunday. We would create a kind of day-conference feel and turn Chorleywood into a campus. Using the centre as well as rooms and halls around Chorleywood, we would go into New Wine mode and offer practical workshops as well as main sessions that served the needs of our people. Now that most of our people were in full mission mode, they needed training 'on the go' – just as Jesus' disciples had. The fifth Sunday would be for refreshment and resourcing. No MSCs would meet that Sunday either.

In the end we empowered people to make their own decision, giving everyone a chance to pray and then choose which of these two options they wanted to take. Some decided to come back and be stationed at the church centre. The majority wanted to stay out in MSCs but come in on certain Sundays.

Having done all this, we prepared for the weekend of the reopening of the church building. We reorganised our congregation into a 'gathered-and-dispersed' church. Once that was done, we asked the MSC leadership teams to decide whether they wanted to come into the centre on any other Sunday besides the fourth Sunday. Some did, so we identified two other Sunday mornings when they could come in for what we came to call a 'network service'. Four or five MSCs come into the centre on one of those Sundays and meet out the other two. Not all MSCs have chosen to come into the centre on the first and second Sundays. Many have decided to meet out three Sundays and come in only on the last Sunday.

Embracing the genius of 'and'

During the time out of the building we had wrestled with the question, 'Is this time out in MSCs a temporary expedient or a long-term strategy?' Initially, before leaving the building, I had written to all the vicars of the parishes where we were setting up MSCs to share what we were doing and ask for their support. Out of all the clergy I wrote to I had three replies. One of them wanted to ask some very legitimate questions. Two of them offered us warm hospitality. As the time went on, however, I began to realise more and more that the majority of the twenty MSCs that we had established (some of which were outside Chorleywood) would not want to disband. They had been released in mission and the gold reserves had been opened. Calling everyone back into the building in September would crush them. And in any case there would not be enough room to accommodate them.

At the same time, I became aware that there were some – albeit a much smaller number – who had not enjoyed the MSC experience and who were simply counting the days until the return to the centre. I had several letters and emails during the nine months from good people I knew and loved, saying that they could not personally buy in to the MSC experience and wanted to resume services at their parish church. These people deserved a home and it was my responsibility to make sure they found one.

In situations like these it is easy to polarise the debate into an either-or situation: either everyone stays out in

MSCs and we use the church building simply for training, or we get everyone back into the building and do away with MSCs altogether. There were people who argued for both. In the end the solution was more inclusive, diverse and complex than either of these simplistic alternatives. The Holy Spirit showed us that the church was supposed to function in a dynamic combination of gathered-and-dispersed expressions. He showed us the need for a strong centre, but also for many smaller expressions of community orbiting in and out of that fixed point in a carefully orchestrated rotation. In short, the Father helped us to find the radical middle between two apparently irreconcilable opposites.

What was created in the process was something that had what Jim Collins would describe as the genius of 'and'. Collins talks in his seminal book *Built to Last* about companies and organisations that stand the test of time and the winds of change. He says that those that fail to last tend to engage in what he calls the tyranny of 'or'. Those that succeed embrace the genius of 'and'. Jim Collins, writing for the business world, says this:

> Instead of being oppressed by the Tyranny of the OR, highly visionary companies liberate themselves with the Genius of the AND – the ability to embrace both extremes of a number of dimensions at the same time. Instead of choosing between A or B, they figure out a way to have both A AND B.

What we ended up with when we returned to the build-ing in September 2005 was a church of the AND, not the OR. Those who wanted to stay out in MSCs were allowed and encouraged to. Those who wanted to come back to the centre to worship there were allowed and encouraged to as well. But those in the dispersed MSCs were asked to make sure they came to our gathered meetings at the centre once a month and to ensure that St Andrew's Church was their true spiritual home. Those at the centre were asked to resource, pray for and support the work of those who had established missional communities in school halls, homeless shelters, community centres, coffee shops and so on. Those who felt called to the centre were also encouraged to join midweek MSCs. This visionary solution gave everyone the opportunity not only of finding a community to belong to, but also of participating in what was increasingly becoming a very vibrant, innovative and effective example of a mission-shaped church. This was a solution we couldn't have dreamed up ourselves. It was self-evidently the Father's dream.

The art of listening

In coming to all these decisions we had to learn as leaders the ability to listen. Leaders are used to speaking. Communication is something leaders have to master. You can't influence other people in the direction God wants them to go unless you have communicational ability. At the same time, leaders have to be really good listeners. They need to be able to hear at a number of different levels.

They need first of all to be able to hear the views of the people they are leading. Leading people through major change will provoke a great deal of comment. This is a sign of life and should not be condemned. People in a volunteer-intensive organisation need to have a voice. That is only right. The leader's responsibility is to make space to hear what is being said, to filter out the destructive comments, and to focus on the constructive, edifying contributions of those who are clearly 'on message' with the vision. This is often hard, because leaders can be oversensitive and those offering views can sometimes be very manipulative. But the art of listening has to be mastered by effective spiritual leaders.

In the time before, during and directly after the nine months of 2005, Drew and I (along with the rest of the leadership) had to learn to listen carefully to the views of others. Of particular importance were the views of our MSC leadership teams. These leaders were very close to all the dispersed members of our church and were best placed to be effective signallers to and from the overall leaders of the church. Of special importance was the time of listening in the summer of 2005, when all but one MSC expressed the desire to continue the experience of meeting out after the refurbishment.

At the same time we had to learn to listen to the Father's voice throughout this process. As we came to endings, as we went through the neutral zone and as we arrived at new beginnings in September 2005, we learned to lean very much on the Father in the storms of change. Indeed, there has rarely been a time in my life when I was not more dependent on the gift of prophecy. This was a time when I couldn't run to a manual, but I could run to Immanuel. This was a season when I was not to lean on my own understanding but rather trust in the Lord with all my heart. Come to think of it, this should be the normal Christian life!

Before we left the building, three prophetic words came my way which proved encouraging. The first was by David Noakes and went like this: 'In the days to come, that part of the church which will survive and prevail will be that part which has learned to walk upon the water, trusting only in me. There will be such storms that it will no longer be possible to cross the waters by ordinary means, for the storms will be such that any

Walk on Water by the Spirit.

boat will founder. The ways of traditional church will not be adequate, because they will be too rigid and inflexible to withstand the wind and the waves. Those who have put their trust in them for security will be like those who find themselves in a boat which is overwhelmed and doomed to sink. In those days only those who have learned to walk upon the waters will walk in safety. Teach my people, therefore, the way of walking on the water. Teach them in these days while the waters are yet calm to fix their eyes upon me with a wholehearted intensity, and to trust me implicitly in all matters, whether they seem great or small.'

This prophecy spoke right into our situation, in which we were teaching the whole church to walk on water.

The second word came from David Orton. He had received a prophecy during the 1990s based on the story of Jesus coming to the disciples, walking on the Sea of Galilee in the midst of the storm. I had not heard it during that decade but it came to my attention just at the time I was preparing my sermon series on 'Walking on Water'. When I read it I knew that the Father was speaking directly to our situation in St Andrew's ten years later.

David Orton prophesied out of Mark 6:45–52 that there was a visitation of the Holy Spirit coming to God's people, but that it was coming from 'outside the boat'. He said that the boat represented the security of our known but outmoded church structures. The storm represented the winds of change that were upon us. Some inside the boat would be afraid and paralysed by their fear. But others would be stirred.

Orton put it like this: 'Some, like Peter, will be stirred in their hearts. And at the word of the Lord they will step out of the boat to come to him. They will be irresistibly drawn from the securities of familiar patterns

and structures to him, and thus, stepping out of them, will enter a new realm of freedom for the miraculous. They will distinguish themselves from the rest of the disciples by their fearless hunger to be with him – to come to him "outside the boat", and thus step into the "new thing". They will be willing to suffer with him outside the city gates, bearing the reproach outside the camp (Heb. 13:12). . . . And so, through this visitation, the church will be purged of human control. The "out-of-church phenomenon" (a trend being commented on by some where many thousands of mature believers have left the institutional structures of the church) is one aspect of this – of the shifts and changes from the old to the new. A visitation is coming from outside the prevailing structures and patterns of the church. It will challenge us as to whether we will go to him outside the boat, or stay within the security of man-made structures. There is a new move coming, so radically different we will all need to step out from where we are. It will be a reformation which turns us from hanging on to our structures to the person of Jesus. We will be faced with the choice of stepping out into his presence or staying with our patterns. The issue is one of control. Will we hang on, toiling in our own strength – or will we let go, fleeing only to him? The choice is ours.'

The third prophetic word came from Kathy Knight, a long-term member of St Andrew's and one of our mission partners. She had a vision of standing in the surf, watching waves. She saw that there had been two previous waves of the Holy Spirit at St Andrew's, one during John Perry's time as vicar (in the 1960s and 70s) and one during Bishop David Pytches' time (in the 1980s and 90s). Now she saw a new wave breaking. She said of this wave, 'This next wave is going to be a missionary wave. In the Old Testament, at the Tower of Babel, then in the

New Testament in the Jerusalem church, God had to dramatically force them to disperse, mostly against their will. Unlike these, it will be a joy at St Andrew's to have a constant movement of its people all the time, back and forth, in and out.' She sensed the Holy Spirit saying to all, 'Catch the wave!'

No doubt some of you by now are feeling quite seasick with all these oceanic metaphors, but to us at the time they were immensely encouraging. They confirmed the rightness of the direction in which we were heading, while at the same time enlarging our vision of the bigger picture. All this has highlighted for us how indispensable prophecy is for spiritual leadership. The prophetic gift enables us to be proactive. Without it, leaders are nearly always stuck in reactive mode.

A new kind of music

And so it was, at the beginning of September 2005, we returned to St Andrew's for the grand reopening of our beautifully refurbished church. We gathered on the Friday evening and marvelled at the work done to the building. Brand new automatic glass doors opened as we entered. A stunning new and spacious foyer greeted us, with a huge painting by Charlie Mackesey depicting the return of the prodigal son to the arms of the Father. In the worship area, there were now chairs instead of pews. Everywhere there were new carpets and brighter lights. In fact, everything seemed lighter and cleaner. The new lighting system (theatre quality) helped create that effect, as did the newly painted walls and the new ceiling effects. The whole church looked brand new – excellent without being excessive. The rooms leading to the lounge and the lounge itself no longer looked embarrassingly dirty and old but were now up to date, multi-functional and thoroughly God-honouring. We had a brand new church. The money (over £800,000) had been raised in one month by the people of St Andrew's. The work had been completed in nine months. Jim Sutton and his team had worked wonders. We gathered and gave thanks to the Lord, rededicating his house and ourselves for the mission ahead, and celebrating the goodness of our Heavenly Father who had kept and blessed us during a quite amazing journey.

We had a brand new church, yes. But the church is not the building. The church is the people. And we had been refurbished too. In fact, we had been radically recalibrated by the experience of being sent out in missional communities. We too – like the building – would never be the same again. We had left behind the old model in which we all stayed in one place and effectively said to the world, 'Come to us.' Instead, we had embraced a new paradigm in which the building was a resource centre for a 'go to them' momentum. Over a thousand people had had a taste of this new model, and the majority had experienced and indeed embraced the paradigm shift, the revolution in thinking that this adventure had elicited. We had learned that the church really is a verb, not a noun. It really is something we are and do, not something we go to.

I started this chapter by describing the first morning in September when I had said, 'Oh no, what have I done?' I had no building to go to, no services to lead, no sermons to preach. Instead, I had to learn a whole new way of leading. Instead of doing it all myself, I had to give it away to others and let them have a go. In the process, I learned that the church was not *leaderless* but *leader-full*. There were potential leaders everywhere, just waiting to be released to express their entrepreneurial spirit in mission. My job changed overnight. Instead of doing most of the preaching, I began to create the notes and the materials to enable nearly one hundred other people to do it. On Sundays I would then go off to hear the inspiring ways in which they taught the Word using their own story. This was a whole new way of leading – and I began to really enjoy it.

Max De Pree has written a brilliant book on leadership entitled *Leadership Jazz*. He compares leading an organisation with being a jazz band leader:

> I enjoy jazz, and one way to think about leadership is to consider a jazz band. Jazz-band leaders must choose the music, find the right musicians, and perform – in public. But the effect of the performance depends on so many things – the environment, the volunteers playing in the band, the need for everybody to perform as individuals and as a group, the absolute dependence of the leader on the members of the band, the need of the leader for the followers to play well. What a summary of an organization!

He follows this with one of the quotations I use most in the training of our leaders here at St Andrew's:

> A jazz band is an expression of servant leadership. The leader of a jazz band has the beautiful opportunity to draw the best out of the other musicians. We have much to learn from jazz-band leaders, for jazz, like leadership, combines the unpredictability of the future with the gifts of individuals.

What happened in 2005 changed my perspective on leadership for ever. Instead of trying to be the virtuoso soloist at the front, driven by the need to perform, I became a jazz-band leader, whose primary task came to be drawing out the latent, God-given creativity in other people. I would provide a basic script for the MSC musicians. But they were then given permission to 'go forth and improvise'. In the process, my role became one of a servant leader, and it produced a brand new kind of music, and a season of new songs.

Jazz enthusiast Nat Hentoff said this about Duke Ellington: 'Ellington talked to me about his music. He composed with each musician in the band particularly in mind. "You keep their weaknesses in your head as you write," he said, "and that way you astonish them with their strengths."' I cannot think of a better description of the change in perspective that I experienced during those history-making months of 2005. We saw ordinary people doing extraordinary things for God. And that joyful trend has only become stronger over the subsequent months.

7

FOLLOWING THE CLOUD

Andrew Williams

As we were preparing to leave the church building in 2005, the Lord made us a promise. As he promised Moses, so he said to us, 'My presence will go with you, and I will give you rest' (Ex. 33:14). There was a season when we did not dare mention the second part of that promise because a lot of our people were working very hard preparing the lifeboats for launch, and every time we mentioned it they would roll their eyes and laugh. But as you would expect, the Lord was and has continued to be faithful to his promise. This is not a strategy where the people of God are to be exhausted in well-doing. Perhaps the worst thing that could ever be said of a church is 'the glory has departed' (1 Sam. 4:21). And yet in this brave new season we were leaving the building to find that the glory of God travelled with us and indeed was waiting for us in the most surprising places. This chapter is an attempt to honour the Lord's commitment to us in keeping his promise.

Naturally supernatural

As we worked together in this new paradigm of dispersed and gathered, we very soon discovered that the presence of God increased. Strange events and godly coincidences are scattered throughout our story. So much so that in January 2007 I prepared a series entitled 'Naturally Supernatural', written with the desire to take the 'flaky' and the 'spooky' out of the supernatural, that we might have a biblical, Jesus-centred focus on the power of the Holy Spirit and the things of the Kingdom of God. In this series we looked at the biblical mandate for angels; the Lord's capacity to speak to us in our dreams; the power of love; visions; healing and even smells and strange events. This may sound like an unusual list of topics but we needed to equip our people biblically in understanding the supernatural things that the Holy Spirit was doing out in the MSCs and at the centre.

During this season the whole church became much more attuned to the Father's voice, including and especially our children. A seven-year-old boy had a dramatic vision in which he encountered the Father in his throne room. He later replicated something of what he saw in Lego! In response to this rising tide, Dave and Julie Hill (now leading the children's work at St Andrew's) began a children's midweek MSC called 'VIP' to help children who wanted to go deeper in their faith. These evenings were very popular with older children and were an intriguingly fruitful source of outreach. In time this MSC multiplied into two MSCs.

The supernatural theme continued in other ways. A baptism candidate awoke to find an angel at the foot of his bed on the morning of his baptism. A room full of MSC leaders witnessed the roar of rushing wind through a closed building as they gathered to worship.

Prayer meetings were sometimes flooded with the scent of roses or vanilla. Thunder quaked, on a fine day and on cue, over St Andrew's church building as the Father's grieving heart for those who do not know him was spoken out. Rainbows appeared over the church. Fine gold dust was visible upon our hands, feet and lips. A lovely lady in our church family was helping to lead a time of worship in her MSC. She was reading from Romans 10:9–10 'That if you confess with your mouth, "Jesus is Lord," and believe in your heart that God raised him from the dead, you will be saved. For it is with your heart that you believe and are justified, and it is with your mouth that you confess and are saved.' She told me, 'When I returned home Harry said to me, "Whatever is that on your lips? Have you been eating a sticky cake?" When I looked in a mirror I could see clearly that it was gold dust which was covering my lips. I touched this but it could not be moved. I said to Harry that I knew what it was but he would not believe me if I told him. Harry said, "Try me." I replied, "Gold dust from heaven." Harry is a scientist and has to have an explanation for everything, but this time he was speechless and truly amazed. The gold dust remained for some time. The next day Harry said, "You have that gold on your lips again." I did for the following five days, and always at the same time, about 12 midday, but not quite so much as that first time. I believe that the Lord wants me to use my lips more in praising and worshipping him and spreading the word.' What particularly thrilled me was that it was Harry, who is not a regular church attender, who first told me of these events at an MSC summer barbecue where he was very much at home. Clearly touched by what had taken place, he finished his story: 'So what do you make of that then?'

And in the MSCs and at the church centre people were healed and people were brought to a living faith in Jesus Christ.

Worship and intercession

There is no prophetic revelation without worship and intercession. Mark had preached a mini-series in 2004 on St Andrew's being an Antioch church. The Antioch church in Acts 13 had ministered to the Lord in worship and intercession, and then the Holy Spirit had ministered to the church in prophetic revelation, instructing the leaders whom to set apart and giving them strategic insight (Acts 13:1–3). We recognised something of this same biblical pattern within our own experience.

Prayer has always been at the core of what we do, but this new paradigm caused intercession to come into renewed importance. Not long after we had returned to the building, a much loved elder statesmen in St Andrew's was called home. Phil Clark had led the intercessory power house of the church for many years alongside his wife Helen, another legend. Without their unfailing commitment, passion and encouragement to the congregation to intercede for the life of the church, we would have no story to tell or at least a very much shorter story. Phil's death was a deep loss felt right across the church family. I recall one particular Sunday morning when Phil was in so much pain that he had propped himself up against the chapel wall while he continued to pray for others, anointing them with oil as they were filled with God's Holy Spirit. The service of thanksgiving for Phil's life was a tremendous witness to the fullness of the Father's love in his life. We all miss him terribly. But in being called home, Phil left us a wonderful legacy. Under Helen's anointed leadership, a new intercessory team came to the fore. All that Phil and Helen had learned and laboured in together was now more widely shared with a team who were committed to pray for the MSCs and for the church.

As well as this team at the centre, each MSC was forming its own prayer group. If you care about what you are doing, if you know the Lord's calling in what you are doing, if you feel just a little bit or a lot out of your comfort zone – you pray. As a whole church, we now have a regular habit of calling forty days of prayer and fasting. Once this might have exhausted us, but now we have MSC teams working with our intercessory team to keep the fire of intercession burning.

I send out weekly emails to all the MSC leadership teams, asking for testimony and prayer requests, and their replies are fed back into the network of intercession. This network of prayer follows a weekly cycle through our own personal prayer lives, midweek prayer meetings and Sunday morning intercessions at the centre. Week by week we see the Lord answering prayer in the most wonderful and creative way and this builds faith and expectancy.

So prayer was important, and so was worship. Worship is of course more than just singing, but nevertheless singing plays an important part in worship. Embarking on the MSC adventure presented us with some major challenges on this front. Where were we to find the minstrels to lead the army, as in Jehoshaphat's day? When developing the MSC strategy I had created a little guide that went something like this. 'Let's say that you have a gift to lead worship. How are you going to grow in that gift? To try to lead worship in your sitting room with half a dozen unmusical friends might not be the most encouraging climate. At the same time, to put someone who is just starting out before the whole congregation is equally unkind.' This always drew a response because everyone knew what this felt like – either as a nervous leader or as a nervous participator. 'MSCs are an environment where you can really learn and thrive in your gifting.' I hoped that this was right. Holy Trinity Brompton had said something similar with reference to their pastorates and it made a lot of sense to me.

Fortunately this was right. It took a while, but in the goodness of community, nervous musicians began to offer their gifts. This was very encouraging, but there was something even more wonderful that I had left out. Musically, worship within MSCs might be a little unpolished. Often it was not as refined as the worship we brought to God at the centre, but out in the community, walking on floors that were sticky with beer, in coffee shops and school halls the Father smiled upon our people's praises; you could palpably sense his presence and his pleasure. It was a recurring testimony: 'The presence of the Lord was with us!'

The dispersed paradigm also brought new creativity to worship. New songs of worship were written. Hand in Hand (our MSC for the deaf) reported, 'We recently had four first-time visitors – but the best moment for me personally was that our worship included a new signed song written by one of our deaf members. I almost cried. How I have longed over the years for this to happen.' One MSC had all its members painting together on the theme of the glory of God. This no doubt came as a bit of a shock to some of the members who had not picked up a paintbrush since their schooldays, but very soon all ages were joined together in little groups working together on a shared piece of art. At the end of the session the works of art were exhibited and became a visual stimulus for the whole group as they spoke out prayers of thanksgiving acknowledging the glory of Jesus.

The Grand, an MSC for the 'twenty-somethings', was full of highly gifted musicians and worship leaders. The Lord had other plans for their talents. In their meetings in Café Nero the management made one prohibition: no live music. They were soon developing models of worship that brought praise to God through visual media, literature, poetry and even taste: the chilli powder and chocolate worship was particularly effective.

Other MSCs were similarly challenged and inspired. Golden Doors, meeting in Starbucks, developed their own worship style; the MSC leaders told us, 'We don't stand on tables and preach to the assembled masses. We don't sing to them either. Over coffee we have highly interactive Bible study. What we do is talk (often quite loudly) about subjects in line with the teaching material. And in the same way we pray: for each other, the church, the neighbourhood and the people in the shop.' On my visits to Golden Doors I was always struck by the way this MSC changed the atmosphere in the coffee house as they brought the Holy Spirit's agenda to the table.

As well as these wonderful times of prayer and praise there was a growing realisation of a truth that we all knew but were now experiencing in a new way: our whole lives were becoming an act of worship to the Lord. MSCs were drawing alongside the communities in which they were meeting in diverse and innovative ways. One MSC, The Anchor, found itself in a village that had seen a category C men's prison built within its boundaries in fairly recent times. As you might imagine, this had not been universally popular among that community. Petitions had been signed, letters written, local councillors and MPs called upon. The prison was nevertheless built. The MSC saw an opportunity to bless the prison community. The Angel Tree project was an existing ministry that had been developed by Prison Fellowship. Its vision was to enable fathers who were spending Christmas at Her Majesty's pleasure to send their children a Christmas present with a handwritten message to be opened on Christmas morning. Two of the MSC members were already supporting this ministry, and now the whole MSC got behind the project. A local businessman and toy entrepreneur offered a range of good-value toys and then warehouse space to store, wrap and pack the parcels. The MSC then set about raising funds to cover the costs. In the course of this they visited local businesses and shops, engaging the wider community in the work. These businesses and shops were very generous. Over three consecutive Christmas seasons 400 gifts grew to 775. That is 775 children who on Christmas morning received the Father's love in the form of a gift from their dad. This turned out to be a record number of gifts across the country for this scheme and their work inspired similar projects in other prisons.

Reporting for the youth MSCs, Pete Wynter told us, 'We mobilised the young people to do a load of social action projects in our community. More than seventy young people turned out, working in nursing homes, doing gardening for elderly neighbours, washing windows, painting fences, giving out lollies, helping at a local school fête and putting on a football tournament. Actions speak louder than words.'

One MSC saw the opportunity to bless a nearby nursing home by offering a traditional afternoon tea to all the residents. As they continued in this ministry they discovered there were elderly people whose birthdays were going unnoticed, so they threw birthday parties for residents, some of whom were well into their nineties. Every member of the MSC sent a birthday card so that there were plenty of cards to open on the special day. Often the outreach was just incredibly practical – one MSC got alongside a local school and gave up their time to sort out the filing. Some members of another MSC befriended a Muslim family in their neighbourhood who had come to the UK having been terribly persecuted in their country of origin. Very shortly afterwards, the whole MSC turned up on their doorstep and performed a garden make-over that the *Ground Force* team would have been proud of. Every member got involved, and at one point one of the team noticed the children washing the worms!

Presence and healing

As the worship and intercession went up to heaven, there were other signs of the presence of the Lord. The Bible teaches us to expect supernatural phenomena as we go out to preach the Gospel: in Mark 16:15–18, Jesus expressly promised that when his disciples go out into all the world to preach good news, signs will follow, that 'they will place their hands on sick people, and they will get well'. And so it was.

On Good Friday 2006, at St Andrew's church centre I watched two of our MSC leaders standing quietly before the cross with a lady who was also a member of their MSC. This lady and I had spent some time together. She had shown tremendous courage in some challenging circumstances but events had taken their toll on her health and she had been ill for a period of about fourteen years. In the last six years her health had deteriorated to the extent that she needed to walk with the aid of crutches. As the three of them stood quietly before the large wooden cross asking the Lord to heal her, their friend received a touch from the King and was healed right in front of them. They called me over. She was beaming and standing without any aid; her crutches were discarded on the floor. I remember asking her incredulously, 'Well, how long have you walked with crutches?' She lifted her arms to show me the calluses on the underside of her hands where over the past six years the crutches had left their mark. This lady is now on the leadership team of the MSC and among many other things has a formidable gift as an administrator. At one time these things would have been quite beyond her, but that Good Friday morning the Lord had promised her, 'I am going to give you hope and a future.' In my view, her story is beautifully illustrative of the love, healing, restoration and release that the Lord was pouring out through the dispersed and gathered network.

MSCs were now filling with people who were attracted by the goodness of the extended family life within that community and who were gently but surely getting to know the love of their Heavenly Father for themselves. One morning two of our church members bumped into a friend and neighbour on the high street. Their neighbour had been along to many of the social events organised by their MSC. On this particular day he was clearly in a lot of pain. He explained that he had woken that morning with excruciating pain in his back and legs. His friends offered to pray for him, and he agreed, no doubt thinking that they would do this later in the privacy of their own home. Right there and then, on the street, they prayed a short and simple prayer for his healing. He thanked them and hobbled home. The next day they were out and about and this time their neighbour came bounding towards them, smiling from ear to ear. He was bursting with the news. He had woken that morning to find his leg lifted in the air. He described how his leg was manipulated in a way that he could not imitate (he had tried afterwards as he puzzled over these events). As all this took place he had felt relief in his leg and back. A few moments later he was standing in his bedroom and all the pain had left him. He had been healed, and a few weeks later he was persuaded to give testimony at the MSC.

Other testimonies of healing were coming in. One MSC reported, 'We prayed for a member who was to have some abnormal cells removed from her breast. Doctors did X-rays pre-operation and could not find the abnormal cells. No operation was needed.' From a youth MSC we received the news, 'A young person who had fallen down the stairs, damaging tendons and muscles, got healed. Before we prayed, he could not move at all on the foot – it was throbbing with pain. After prayer he put down his crutches and walked freely. He moved the ankle round and round and said that the pain had all gone except for his toe!'

Presence and prophecy

St Andrew's has been blessed over the years by the ministry of some very prophetic people. John Wimber's contribution in the 1980s was a very formative time for St Andrew's and for the wider church. From that same stream St Andrew's was immensely blessed to receive a good friend and prophetic mentor, John Paul Jackson. John Paul is a man of the Word and the Spirit with an international ministry spanning over thirty years. At Mark's invitation, John Paul visited St Andrew's Church in 2002 (the year before I arrived) and during that visit he and his colleague, Mitch, gave St Andrew's an intriguing prophetic word. Prophetically they anticipated a time when St Andrew's would be like a Baskin-Robbins ice cream store; an ice cream parlour with thirty-two unique and delicious flavours of ice cream. At the time this word was not immediately understood – especially since Baskin-Robbins is famous for thirty-one, not thirty-two, flavours – but two years later it had become very evident. By that time we were no longer a church meeting in one place but a network of mission communities with many different and distinctive 'flavours', yet all part of the one St Andrew's Church. We were in fact a Baskin-Robbins church!

By November 2005, the refurbishment was completed and John Paul paid St Andrew's another visit. By this time we were mobilised in over twenty MSCs, each one distinctive in its mission. We realised the number thirty-two in John Paul's prophecy was also important: on our current trajectory of growth and creativity we could see that we would very soon exceed thirty-two 'flavours', and his word was a sign that we were not to put limits on this strategy.

During John Paul's 2005 visit we arranged an evening for all our MSC leaders to meet with him. Before John Paul got up to speak, he squeezed my leg very hard with a friendly but vice-like Texan grip, and with a twinkle in his eye said, 'You are going to love this!' The following is an extract from a prophetic word that John Paul shared with us that night:

> God has been developing an orbital model in you and you did not even notice. He is clever. Now why would he do that to you? Because he says, this is the coming model and he chose you to be a prototype. He wants you to be a demonstration model that churches will come to look at to find out how this model of leadership and church growth operates. The wonderful thing is that this

is non-age-specific. It can work for the youth. It can work for the elderly. It can work for the baby boomers. All of these can work. Then when you come together – wow! There is synergy! You have the opportunity to develop something so 'unchurchy'; it won't offend, it will attract people to Jesus but it will be different, and that is what will attract them. That is why they will love it. With great intent God designed this; with great intent. It will allow things to happen that have never been thought to be able to happen in a church setting before. Now nothing is off-limits, because the mould has been broken.

As our people were growing in their faith, there was a corresponding increase in listening for and hearing the Lord's voice. If you ask the question, 'What is the Lord saying to you?' people are going to listen with much greater intent. Choosing a name for a new MSC was always an encouraging exercise in prayer. Immediately the Lord's creative inspiration would help the new team to find a name that captured something of the heart of the mission objective that the Lord had set them. And then there was the question of where they should meet. Time and time again, a prophetic word, a Bible verse or a picture would lead a new MSC to find the location of the Lord's choosing.

This was dramatically illustrated by the leadership team within the 'WD3' MSC (so named because of the postcode area it was serving). My brother Paul and his wife Alessandra had been part of the leadership team at WD3 until the Lord called Paul to ordination and to plant a church in Maceío, northern Brazil. The MSC was wonderfully supportive in sending them out. One of Paul's many challenges was to find a building, and as the search continued Paul would send me photographs of possible sites. We would pray hard, but for one reason or another these sites were not right. Members of WD3 met to pray for Paul and the location of the new church building, and as they prayed one of the team sensed the Lord's still, small voice whisper, 'Cobbles and bread.' This made no sense to anybody but they faithfully emailed it back to Brazil. That very day, Paul and Alessandra had been out to look at a new building. In a busy neighbourhood, surrounded by towering blocks of apartments, was a single-storey building set in its own garden. There was space to build an area for worship, and the house could easily be adapted to provide facilities for children and youth, prayer, administration and cooking. It was a highly unusual site and an exciting find for Paul and Alessandra. They went home to seek the Lord and were thrilled to receive the email from WD3. The building they had found was set on a cobbled street, immediately next to a bread shop. I have since been to Brazil to visit Paul and have walked the cobbled street and sat in the new church garden where early in the morning the air is filled with the aroma of fresh bread.

Presence and community

I have recently come across some statistics that demonstrate that the modern Briton is an isolated creature. Seventy per cent of us have no ties to any local group or association. It is one of the greatest fallacies of modern life that we were born to be independent. Avoid the crowd. Do your own thinking. Be the chess player and not the chess piece. The Austrian author and journalist Karl Kraus put it rather miserably: 'The world is a prison in which solitary confinement is preferable.'

So in such a culture, not surprisingly, when we think of 'one' our first instinct is to think: singular, mono, separate, alone, independent from. When Jesus speaks about 'one' he has something very different in mind. We should have seen it coming. Biblically, five loaves of bread and two fish have always equalled five thousand plus. With the Lord a day is like a thousand years, and a thousand years are like a day. God is, after all, Father, Son and Holy Spirit – three in one, one in three.

In Kingdom mathematics 'one' is most often plural. One is connected. One is familial. One is community. Notice the Kingdom addition in Jesus' prayer for us: Jesus prayed, 'My prayer is not for them alone. I pray also for those who will believe in me through their message, that all of them may be one, Father, just as you are in me and I am in you' (Jn. 17:20–21). Paul summarises the equation: 'In Christ we who are many form one body, and each member belongs to all the others' (Rom. 12:5).

In a culture of radical autonomy we have often confused a personal faith with an individualistic faith and so community has been jettisoned. Indeed, we often perceive the community of Christ as optional or even as an obstacle. Yet we are baptised into Christ and joined with his body. Every believer passes through the waters of baptism and is drawn into the river of God. Alone we are standing in a puddle. Community remains the Lord's preferred means by which his love may be mediated to us and through us. As we went on this adventure of mission in community we found ourselves within an oasis where those searching for genuine love and acceptance could come and drink deeply.

The concept of 'the many who are one' has a long biblical provenance. The people of God have been working it out for a very long time. In the Old Testament we see a threefold social structure, with three levels of community. First there was the tribe (*sebet/matteh*). Tribe was the primary unit of social and territorial organisation. Tribe was important in time of war, when the military tax was levied by tribe. Tribe was fundamental to a person's identity, but for social purposes it was the least significant of the three levels. Then there was the clan (*mis-paha*). In the Old Testament the clan was a grouping of families. Marriages were usually made within a clan, in order to preserve land ownership. Clans were important for territorial identity. Boundary lists in Joshua 12–17 were 'allotted to them' (Joshua 14:1) according to their clans. But the third and most significant unit of community was the extended family, comprising all the descendants of a single living ancestor. This would be a group of people sharing their lives in community. It was known as 'the father's house' (*bet' ab*) and it was a person's most important means of identity. Your *bet' ab* was where you belonged, where you were protected, included and had responsibility. And in the early days of the New Testament church it was this third unit that persisted as community. Here it was referred to by the Greek work *oikos*, but this was equivalent to the father's house of the Old Testament, except that this community included not only relatives but also your 'kin in the faith' – slaves, employees, business clients and friends. These communities were as large as the largest room in the largest house and they were the place where three things happened: conversion (Cornelius in Acts 10), worship and discipleship (Acts 2:46, 5:42, 12:12). It is even possible to trace Paul's missionary strategy through these mid-sized groupings: Lydia and the jailor both provided something approaching an MSC in Philippi (Acts 16:15, 31–34), as did Stephanas, Crispus and Gaius in Corinth (Acts 18:8; 1 Cor. 1:14–16), Priscilla and Aquila and Onesiphorus in Ephesus (1 Cor. 16:19; 2 Tim. 1:16; 4:19), Philemon at Colossae (Phlm. 1–2), Nympha at Laodicea (Col. 4:15) and Aristobulus, Narcissus and company in Rome (Rom. 16:10–11).

For St Andrew's, MSCs had become something comparable to the Father's house. In the fixed purpose of mission, MSCs said: you do belong, you are loved, you are valued, you have a destiny in Jesus Christ and together we are going to work that out.

In all the supernatural activity of the Holy Spirit, the miracle of authentic Christian community was now being rediscovered. It was as if increasing the surface area of the church through the diaspora of MSCs gave our people a greater opportunity to love their neighbour. Erwin McManus explains, 'Love compels us to community; love calls us to each other. It is not about loving people who are always easy to love; it is about loving people through the love of God.' And communities that have this capacity are deeply attractive because they reveal Jesus.

Pastoral care went to a new level as church members were being loved and cared for within the MSCs. Like any vicar, I was accustomed to receiving telephone calls telling me that one of our members was unwell, that there was some sudden crisis or that a loved one had died. If they were sick, we would find out which hospital they were in, if they were allowed visitors or if they were being visited at all. Now, when the telephone rang, we would also contact the MSC leader. Time and time again, I would very soon be in receipt of a visiting schedule prepared by the MSC, showing which members would be visiting their sick friend over a period of time. Days of prayer and fasting were quietly arranged in much the same way. One MSC went to the lengths of organising a cooking and laundry plan for a sick member's elderly mother.

In times of bereavement, MSCs were able to comfort and support those who grieved in a very sensitive and loving way. There was constancy in their love that brought healing and hope. David and Jenny recall a morning when they visited an MSC where a much-loved family member had very suddenly died. That Sunday, the bereaved wife bravely came along to the MSC gathering. The MSC suspended their plans and spent the time praying for her and for the family, each member sharing what her husband had meant to them. David later commented that much as we would have liked to, we would have been unable to care for someone in quite this way in a usual Sunday service.

Another much-loved member of the St Andrew's church family was unwell for quite some time. Eventually it was necessary for him to be cared for in a nursing home. His wife's MSC supported her through this difficult time, providing lifts to the nursing home, taking her husband communion and bringing prayer and worship to his bedside. The MSC became a safe place where she could draw strength and shed some tears. When the Lord called her husband to be with him, the MSC sensitively supported her with the funeral arrangements, leading the worship at the thanksgiving service and even supplying the catering. The MSC remains a family that supports her and cherishes her husband's memory.

Through a signing interpreter, Julian Nuttall gave testimony to the whole church about his MSC, telling us, 'Hand in Hand for me is like a second home. My wife and I were looking for a deaf church. Where is it, where is it? We found it here. It was an integrated congregation – we were so happy – with deaf people who could share the experience of worshipping and praise all together. Before, I felt like my relationship with Jesus had gone. But now, I'm back, straight on track. I'm happy. Lots of deaf people, they're all isolated, like I was before. They don't know Jesus, they're far away. They have to travel a long way. I want to see Hand in Hand grow, and encourage deaf people to come – to take on responsibility for something. We feel God wants us to move to Watford, because that's where the deaf community is – in that place.'

The hole in the fence

When I was a child the only Christians I knew lived on the opposite side of the road to us. Quite deliberately we never had anything to do with them. I did not meet or speak with these neighbours for over thirty years – until recently I met them again in a sodden field at New Wine's CLAN Gathering at St Andrew's in Scotland. They said, 'You probably don't remember us, but we lived opposite your house when you and your brother were little boys. We just wanted to say hello and to tell you that all those years ago we prayed so hard for you and your brother and your family.' This had been a very unhappy time for us as a family, and to know that the Father was looking out for us in a season that felt so dark really moved me. Our former neighbour asked me if I remembered his Alsatian: I did. He said, 'I used to walk my dog late at night so that I could walk past your home and pray for you and your brother. We could see all the pain and it felt like there was nothing we could do, but we knew the Lord was calling us and our fellowship to pray for you.'

I asked them if I could share something with them from that same time in my life. Over thirty years ago, as a ten-year-old boy making my way home one Saturday evening, I took a short cut through a track that ran to the side of their back garden. It was a summer's evening and I could hear laughing and music, so I stopped and looked through a hole in their garden fence to see what was going on. I could see a group of about twenty or thirty people in the back garden enjoying each other's company. I remember that I was utterly transfixed by what I saw. I think I stood there for over half an hour watching them. There was something different about the way they talked and laughed together. There was a kindness in their being together that I had not seen before. I was ten years old, I knew nothing about Jesus, but I knew that these people were Christians and I desperately wanted to be with them on the other side of that fence.

At St Andrew's, over the past four years we had seen an increase in the supernatural activity of God. We had witnessed miracles and encountered many touches from heaven. But just as powerful as any single miracle we had witnessed was the miracle of Christian community, where those who are searching for the love of God find Jesus through the love of God's people. Jesus said, 'A new command I give you: Love one another. As I have loved you, so you must love one another. By this all men will know that you are my disciples, if you love one another' (Jn. 13:34–35). The miracle of Christian community was breaking out across the MSC network and people who were looking through holes in fences were being drawn in by cords of loving kindness.

Presence and transformation

Every week I send all the MSC leaders an email which we have come to know and love as the 'MSC Mini-bite'. These Mini-bites are a message of godly encouragement to the troops, and in response the MSC leaders send back some testimony and their prayer requests. Testimony is widely used in a variety of ways to encourage all of us. The prayer requests are fed into the prayer network.

Week by week we would receive news of new people joining an MSC, of people returning to the Lord and of the MSCs being places where people were giving their lives to Jesus for the first time. Haven MSC (working with the homeless) was going from strength to strength. The Lord was adding to their number week by week and the leadership team was expanding. Here is a Mini-bite from Haven in early 2006:

> One of our members came with six new people, including a lady. After we had prayed and finished with a final song of worship there were requests for an encore; we praised God way past our usual finish time! When we offered the group the opportunity to pray our 'Come home' prayer, the new lady said she wanted to give her life to Jesus. With tears of joy and repentance she prayed, while the others encouraged and affirmed her. She said, 'At last I have hope.' She looked so beautiful and peaceful as she left. Praise God! What a privilege to be entrusted with His work.'

Danielle is a member of Haven MSC and her testimony is told very movingly in Janet Hosier and Liza Hoeksma's excellent book *Entertaining Angels*. Danielle begins her story: 'I don't remember any good part of my childhood; in fact I don't suppose I was a child for very long as my upbringing hardly protected my innocence. My mum was 16 when I was born; my dad had already cleared off and though I know his name, that's all I know about him.' Danielle's family life broke down and she was placed in a children's home, then fostered by a woman who was an alcoholic and introduced her to drink and drugs. This was all before Danielle was fourteen years of age. Danielle was sent to a rehabilitation centre where, as she recounts, attempts were made to help her physically but her deep emotional and spiritual wounds were simply unmet. Not surprisingly, the treatment was unsuccessful. Danielle was thrown out of the centre and comments, 'I felt lost and worthless.' Having reached rock bottom, Danielle was then introduced to some Christians who were themselves reformed addicts and who were operating a twelve-step recovery programme. With their encouragement, she says, she first began to pray. Danielle describes the events that followed:

> Darren, who is a recovering alcoholic, lives in the house and he'd become a Christian at the church held in the New Hope Day Centre [Haven MSC]. He invited me to his baptism at St Andrew's Church and it all began to make sense to me. When I walked through the door I felt at home; tears and pain came to the surface, but that felt good and healthy as for so long they'd been repressed. I realised that I wanted to say to God that I wanted him to have all of me, that I wanted to be all that he wanted me to be. I had been living in darkness, but I wanted to live in the pure light that Jesus was offering me. It felt like making a marriage vow. I was certain about what I wanted; I made a commitment that night to hand my life over to the will and care of God. It's early days in my faith, but I am learning loads and it's made my path to recovery much clearer. Since then I've been going to the church at the day centre [Haven MSC] and I love it. . . . Now I know that I am a child of God and that he loves me. I'll always be an addict but I believe I can stay off the drugs and make something of my life.

This recovered sense of identity as a child of God was visible across the whole church in every MSC and within the hearts of those who were supporting the strategy from the centre. In November 2006 we had a Vision Sunday, where the MSC vision was celebrated. We asked members of each MSC to give testimony of how their lives had changed in God since we had begun this adventure together. Many people were willing to participate, across all ages of the church family. We equipped each MSC member with a large piece of cardboard and on one side they wrote, using a handful of words, what life had been like before MSCs and then on the reverse side they wrote how the Lord had changed them in this new season. Here is what they said:

Called from 6009 miles away to be ready/**Now in service, challenged and growing**

Shackled to past/**Freed to purpose**

Secure in known/**Excited out of the boat**

Empty life/**Full of the Holy Spirit**

Pew-warmer/**God's worker**

Sitting on the premises/**Standing on the promises**

Broken/**Restored**

My Way/**Yahweh**

God's Kingdom on Earth . . . watching it happen/ **. . . making it happen**

Isolation/**Belonging**

Being on my own/**Being part of a family**

Coasting along/**Developing gifts**

Limited opportunity/**Opportunity to share in family**

No vision/**Vision**

Blowing in the wind/**Anchored and safe**

Lost and alone/**Found and befriended**

Without direction/**Accepted, loved and secure**

Isolated and alone/**Involved and belonging**

Lost and directionless/**Purposeful**

Hurting, unloved and imprisoned/**Healed, loved and free**

Rejected and unwanted/**Chosen and special**

Empty/**Filled**

Felt lost in numbers/**Now closer and intimate**

Anonymous/**In a family**

Cancer/**Healed by God's grace**

Jesus and me/**Jesus and my loving family**

Limited fellowship/**Increased fellowship**

In need/**Answered prayer**

Sickness/**True happiness through community**

Hard times/**Trusting the Lord**

Worried about eternity/**With Jesus for ever**

Darkness/**Sunlight**

Slavery and hatred/**Freedom and loved**

Ignorance/**Wisdom**

Lonely/**Part of God's amazing family**

Selfish Tim/**Saved by Jesus**

Knew only one person in Watford/**Widened group of
friends**

Lost (but didn't know it)/**Saved (and
knows it)**

Spoon-fed/**Feeding myself**

Abandoned/**Owned by God**

God: 'The Authoritarian'/**God: 'My Daddy'**

Had eczema/**Healed**

Always worried/**God's got it under control**

Hungry for God/**Sees visions of his glory**

Anxiety/**Relaxed**

No faith/**Full of faith**

Boundaries/**Freedom**

Fear held me prisoner/**Hope set me free**

Darkness/**Light**

Lies/**Truth**

Self-centred/**God-centred**

Living in fear/**Living in his strength**

Unprepared/**Ready**

Still/**Sparkling**

Weak/**Strong, confident**

Unnoticed pew-filler on fringe/**Welcomed participator in family**

We captured the evening service testimonies on DVD, and although I have seen this film many times neither Mark nor I can watch it without being moved. We know and love these people and we also know something of the stories that these few words represent.

At the same time we were also beginning to see how these individual testimonies were rebuilding the church. Every ounce of praise, prophecy, healing, salvation and transformation was producing an unstoppable momentum that was increasing the church's corporate capacity to love and to serve. The MSCs and the centre were now working together in an unprecedented way. Responding to a weekly MSC Mini-bite, our youth pastor Pete Wynter recently emailed me this report concerning

'Th3D', the network of youth MSCs that Pete has built with his team of gifted young leaders. These youth MSCs come together for a large celebration service on Friday nights:

This weekend I have seen an MSC church in full flow, and it fills me with the expectation that the good news of Jesus actually might make it out of the four walls of the church and bring real and lasting change to our area, this nation and the world! Are you ready for this?

On Thursday night we spoke to Breakout [a meeting of Youth MSCs for school years 10 to 13] about developing missional vision for the MSCs that are being re-formed in January. The feedback we got was brilliant and I am confident that we have a group of teenagers who are up for getting the message of Jesus to their friends; the potential is massive and is ready to be released in a new way!

Friday night saw another overwhelming Th3D: young people released into gifting and exercising what can only be described as Holy Spirit-inspired authority. One young lady preached and was exceptional, not only in delivery but in spiritual maturity – how can God craft something so strong and magnificent in someone so young? The worship band was made up of members of the Acts community (11–14s) who played with 'genius' levels of skill, but all had hearts totally focused on God and desiring to meet with him. One of our young guys co-led the worship for the first time and brought a real honesty and integrity as he sang his heart out before our incredible God! Th3D was followed by an all-night of prayer which was really well attended, including a young man of twelve years of age who couldn't wait to spend the night with God, having become a Christian at Resonate [an annual summer camp for all the Youth

MSCs]. We read the entire book of Acts out loud together (five chapters at the beginning of each hour) and used this as a springboard to pray for the church and the youth. A lasting impression from the night is twelve prayer warriors walking around the streets of Chorleywood at 3 am, arms outstretched, blessing and praying for each home and for revival to come on the streets of this town!

On to Saturday, when we took fifteen members of 3DFC [a lads' football MSC] in a minibus to Oxford, to play against a team set up with the same purpose as 3DFC by one of our former members who has gone 'on mission' to Oxford (with a degree to do on the side). The rain fell and the match was drawn but it was a great time for community-building and deepened individual relationships with people who would never darken the doors of a church usually. We were also able to encourage them to attend the activities and services over Christmas.

On Sunday morning I was invited by the team at WD3 MSC to go and do a worship workshop for the older children there. I took three of our youth to help this happen – they all spoke a bit and gave top tips about leading worship – mind-blowing to see a thirteen-year-old teaching 9–11s about how important it is not to be proud and to recognise that we are doing this for God, not as some kind of performance. I was mightily encouraged by what I saw, but most encouraging was the discussion I had with a young lad travelling with me on the way home. He saw and communicated the vision of MSCs without realising what he was saying really; his comments were along the lines of the following: 'When I walked in I felt so at home – they are like a big family, aren't they? When that woman at the front asked for people to give boxes of chocolates to give out to the neighbours for Christmas I almost put up my hand with everyone else – imagine if one of those neighbours comes to WD3, becomes a Christian and then tells all their family and they all become Christians! I can't believe this is happening in all the MSCs all over the place!'

In the evening I arrived at Bethlehem [a reconstruction of first-century life in that town, complete with market and stable, in the interior of St Andrew's] – another unbelievable effort from the centre to resource the church with something excellent. I walked in to the buzz in the building that was packed out. The service was stunning, moving me to worship the Lord with tears (not uncommon as I know I'm a cry baby!).

Somehow this church is doing the best of both worlds in order to reach the lost, and it is a privilege to be a part of it. All this has the danger of sounding like we are perfect, which we all know we are not, but what I have witnessed this weekend is a people taking hold of the hand of Christ and stepping out to see his story known and proclaimed, lived out and experienced. We are part of a movement that is changing the lives of individuals, and transforming the communities in which we live by ushering in the fullness and goodness of the Kingdom of God. What stuns me even more is that all this is only what I saw this weekend. Imagine all the other stuff that was happening that I couldn't see because I can't be in more than one place at a time! Lord, continue to breathe life and inspiration as we follow you in this adventure. (Pete Wynter, December 2007)

On the anvil

You can't expect to be part of a story like this and not to be changed. As all that has been described above (and more) was unfolding, the Lord continued to pin me to the anvil and then quite unexpectedly sent me to New England for a thorough hammering. When John Paul visited St Andrew's at the end of 2005, Elena and I were delighted to have Patty Mapes come and stay with us. Patty and her husband Greg have worked closely with John Paul for many years. Over breakfast, Patty said, 'Hey, here's a thought – you should come out and visit us in New Hampshire in the New Year.' Patty is a woman of her word and within a few emails I was booked to fly out to Boston in February 2006.

You may have seen the Disney/Pixar movie *The Incredibles*. The Incredibles are a superhero family with superpowers who covertly save people from peril and danger. It turned out that the Mapes are the original Incredibles. They don't tell you this; I had to work it all out but I received a clue the moment I landed in Boston. They piled me into the largest 4x4 I have ever seen. Actually it was more like a 16x16. They said, 'We know that for you it is about two in the morning – but we are going to get you through the jet lag as quickly as we can, so we are going to keep you awake, take you out to dinner and buy you a large steak! This is a little tradition we have.' What could I say?

Greg and Patty have four incredible kids. I spent quite a bit of time with their eldest son, Zach. Let me tell you about my friend Zach. When Zach was just five years old he would be out playing in the sandpit and would put down his bucket and spade, walk over to a nearby adult, speak to them prophetically, recite several verses from the Bible that would speak into that person's life and then return to his bucket and spade. All the members of the family share this natural prophetic gifting. And they are really fun people; they have such an appetite for life and for the Lord and the most extraordinary capacity to love. Where others would see insurmountable challenge they see glorious God-given opportunity.

This was not my first trip to the States but it was the first time I had been there as a Christian, so I think I saw things a little differently. Driving around New Hampshire, we would pass through places that have their original namesake in the UK. This was New England after all – clearly English settlers migrated and called their new homes after the place where they had originated. We saw a sign for a place that I recognised as a small market town in Devon. I said, 'I cannot imagine that there were ever any people from that town in England who woke up one morning in the middle of Devon and said, "Ere, let's get on a boat and go live in 'America!'"' Zach replied, 'Well maybe all the guys from that town who had all that get-up-and-go got up and left.' He was teasing but I heard what he said.

Later that night we were watching a cartoon when suddenly on the screen there was a caricature of Hugh Grant. In a very funny English accent he was saying, 'Well, erm, what I mean is . . . what I rather meant to say was . . . in other words . . . sorry – look, the thing is, . . . erm . . .' Zach's brother Duncan said, 'You had an empire, you helped to birth science, industry, theatre and commerce and so much of the arts – you guys were the original global missionaries – you took the Gospel to the world. How did you get from Winston Churchill to Hugh Grant?'

Being around the family, I was aware of the closeness of their walk with the Lord. I was a Spirit-filled Christian and I was not unfamiliar with my Father's voice, but my mindset was that from time to time, if the Lord so chose, he might speak to me. What was becoming apparent was that my Heavenly Father was speaking to me all the time but I was often not listening. Driving around New England, I distinctly heard the Lord's challenge: 'Drew, why are you not walking in the fullness of all that I have given you and called you to?' There was a part of me that was even just a little bit indignant about this. I have been very zealous for the Lord God Almighty – if you had not noticed! But throughout my stay the Lord persisted with this theme, making his point in a variety of ways.

One of them came via Zach's sister Anna. Anna has a superpower that involves basketball; and lots of it. She is in her school first team and they practise every day and all weekend. They are tipped to win the High School league. Now it may be that I went to the wrong school, but when I was at school if there was a league game for any sport with a midweek fixture, you couldn't be sure that someone would turn up to turn the lights on. Not so in America. Now remember, this is a midweek High School league – these players are just sixteen years old. Before you arrive there are hot dogs, doughnuts, candy, sodas and a programme that gives you the form on each player. The bleachers were packed with parents who genuinely wanted to be there. They had three referees plus two guys in a leatherette electronic score booth with hooters. They begin with the national anthem, for which everyone stood and everyone sang. Then the cheerleaders came on and did their thing, after which the two teams came out, crashing through a paper wall accompanied by a smoke machine and strobe lighting. We were not even nearly started. Three of the girls were about to graduate, so they came to the front and the coach said a few nice words about each of them. Their parents came forward and one by one they were presented with flowers; everyone wept. I had never met them, but my goodness, it was all very moving. By this time I needed a lie-down and a strong cup of tea, but then the guy in the leatherette score booth sounded his hooter and the game actually started.

There was just so much energy, commitment, zeal and all-out win-or-die, blood-pumping passion. It was incredible. Zach was filling me in on the finer details but he could not say too much because he was videoing the whole thing so that the team could analyse their game afterwards.

Actually, Anna's team lost. A bit unfortunate really. In the heavy analysis that went on afterwards they came to the conclusion that they had lost because they had spent too much time passing to one another and not shooting for the basket. The team needed to be bolder, to seize the moment and take more risks. I had that sinking sense that the Lord might have been saying something.

A few days later the Lord resumed his conversation and turned the volume way up. Patty said to me, 'Andrew, do you know that the Lord holds you in really high regard?' I said, 'Really?' She said, 'Yes, and my prayer for you in this trip is that you would see this for yourself and that you would walk in the fullness of all that the Lord has called you to.' Patty asked some more questions and I confessed what the Lord had been saying. She smiled and said, 'You need to believe and act upon what God has set in your heart and not fear godly ambition.' She added, 'What is so wrong with saying I want to be a disciple for Jesus rather than to say I just met him once?'

Just before I left on the Sunday a snow blizzard set in. I had never seen this type or quantity of snow before. It fell horizontally. In the UK this would have been a crisis. Everything was made white – so much snow that the snowploughs could not leave the snow at the side of the road but had to take it to dumping stations. We had planned to go to church that morning but the roads, at least to my eyes, were impassable, dangerously impenetrable. So what do the Incredibles do? Greg fired up the 16x16 – with the heated leather seats – and we went to Dunkin' Donuts for coffee and doughnuts. There is a full-scale Arctic blizzard – it is about minus 9 degrees – and we are in Dunkin' Donuts drinking latte and eating frosted doughnuts. Fantastic – I really love these people. And then we went to church.

We arrived at church; blizzard conditions continuing. I thought, obviously, we are going to get there and the service will have been cancelled. But no, the car park was full. As we came in they were in the midst of worship, singing, 'How great is our God'. I was immediately aware that I could hear the angels singing. This was not imagined. Not some sugar-induced hallucination, not even some kind of inner listening. This was a full blown, in your face – out there – up there – angelic chorus. I was lost in love, wonder and praise. As the worship soared around me, I spoke to the Lord. I said, 'You are an incredible God, an incredible Father – thank you for bringing me into the orbit of this incredible family.' The Lord then spoke very clearly. 'And you, son, are incredible too.' I was so shocked I could not sing. My shoulders shook.

After the worship I was introduced to the pastor, Bill. He immediately embraced me, held me very tightly and prayed a blessing over me as he wept: 'Thank you for this man, thank you for bringing him here. Thank you for the calling upon his life.' Then he kissed me on the cheek and I saw that his eyes were ablaze with light. They were all blue – scarcely the hint of a pupil – just all blue light. Greg Mapes took me by the arm and walked me to the front of the hall. 'I think it is important that our ministry team pray for you.' I sat before three people who had no idea who I was or where I was from. What they prayed that day was recorded, and here is a small extract: 'You have been embarking on the new things . . . you are a frontier man, you are a spiritual pioneer and God is going to take you to uncharted territories to find people that have not been reached.'

Why did the Lord take so much trouble over me during this trip? Clearly, there were some very large strongholds within me that were being demolished. So much of this had to do with fear of godly ambition. The largest part of this false piety had everything to do with me but there was also something from within the institution that fed this condition of the heart. There are many inspiring, courageous and prophetic voices within the Anglican house and there are a great many reasons to be encouraged, but there is also a dim but discernible voice that exhorts its church leaders to reject all ambition, to embrace poverty and to manage decline with humility. I am deeply unimpressed by the cult of Christian celebrity. Jesus warned, 'Watch out! Be on your guard against all kinds of greed; a man's life does not consist in the abundance of his possessions' (Lk. 12:15). But the Father has always employed scandalously profligate means to rescue and transform humanity. My stay with the Incredibles was hugely important for me because my Father made it plain that his plans for his church are ambitious and extravagant and that, if we are willing, we all have a part in this adventure. I wrote in my prayer journal, 'I can hear you, Father, I can hear you, I can hear you!'

Returning to the UK

Across the historical breadth of the Bible and two thousand years of church history there has been a continuous stream of men and women, communities and nations that for a season, for the outworking of another chapter in the Lord's great history of salvation, held the baton. Lou Engle captured this responsibility in the grace of God when he wrote, 'There are moments in history when a door for massive change happens. Great revolutions for good or evil occur in the vacuum created by these openings. It is in these times that key men and women, even entire generations, risk everything to become the hinge of history – the pivotal point to determine which way the door will open.'

My time in New England had been Jesus' encouragement to throw off any lingering English reserve and any institutional grave-clothes and to fully embrace his calling. As I squared up to the measure of this responsibility, I could see that the same revelation was also sweeping across the church. It was becoming so evident (to quote Marianne Williamson) 'that the children of God were truly brilliant, gorgeous, talented and fabulous after all and who were we not to be? Our playing small was not going to save the world. There was nothing enlightened about our shrinking so that other people would not feel insecure around us. We were meant to shine as children do. And as we let our own light shine we were unconsciously giving other people permission to do the same.' Corporately, the penny had dropped. 'We were all born to make manifest the glory of God that is within us.'

As we approached the end of 2006 there was so much to give thanks for and to celebrate as church growth and creativity in mission went to new heights. We were seeing growth in every part of our mission as a church, gathered and dispersed. As a whole company we were now around 1,400 people strong, and growing. The children's department was running out of space. Our children were telling us that they loved their MSCs. The youth department was building MSCs as fast as they could find new leaders. All of the MSCs were growing in maturity and in number. There was growth at the centre – numerically and in understanding a new identity as a resourcing centre. In the hands of an assiduous and discerning missional leadership team, there were now the beginnings of what we hoped would be a new network of midweek MSCs under the name Affinity. We had more musicians and more new songs of worship. The prayer ministry team, intercessory team and pastoral visiting team were all thriving. As a gathered-and-dispersed network, working together, we were able to minister to toddlers, children, young people, students, the elderly, adults with learning difficulties, prisoners, the homeless, international communities, the deaf, and neighbourhoods and workplaces covering an expanding geographical area. We were working with mission partners in Eastern Europe, Africa, Pakistan and South America who were in turn planting churches, building Christian schools, fighting AIDS, addiction and poverty. But for me, the most significant part in our story thus far was that the whole body of Christ at St Andrew's – gathered and dispersed – had acknowledged that we served a limitless God who had placed a large and urgent calling upon the life of his church. There was just no getting around it, the love of God was vast and so the commission would always be great.

8

KEEPING THE GLUE STRONG

Mark Stibbe

I have always held unity as a supreme value. In my view, the vicar of an Anglican church is supposed to be a focus of unity. It is the vicar's task to keep everyone together as the church moves forward in mission. Of course, this is all very well in theory, but in practice it is demanding and often messy, especially when you're overseeing a large network of dispersed communities.

Having studied English Literature as my first degree, I tend to use literary allusions a lot in my speaking and writing. One very powerful poem I remember studying in my undergraduate days was 'The Second Coming' by William Butler Yeats. This contains some very memorable and often-cited lines:

Things fall apart; the centre cannot hold;
Mere anarchy is loosed upon the world

In the year after moving back into the building in September 2005, I thought about Yeats' words a lot. Drew and I had seen God's people released in mission and we had grown phenomenally in the process. We were well on our way to being a church of thirty-two flavours – a church with thirty-two different expressions of our church's vision. We had many new mission-shaped communities meeting in all sorts of unchurched contexts. We had broken out of our box and were now experiencing what missiologist Roland Allen once described as 'the spontaneous expansion of the church'. The brakes had been removed and God's people were flying in highly creative expressions of Christian mission. It was a truly exciting season.

At the same time it was somewhat scary. Three Sundays a month we now had many more people out in mid-sized communities than we did at the centre. In fact we were moving quickly to a situation where the majority of the church met most Sundays outside the building in mission mode and one quarter met at the home base. This was not an ecclesiological model that I had seen before and I was confronted by many unprecedented challenges. Of all these challenges the most stretching was this: how do you keep the whole thing together? How do we remain united when we are not just gathered but dispersed? How do I prevent the centre from collapsing and mere anarchy being loosed? In the end, a number of factors have proved extremely important for creating cohesion in this great movement of mission. In this chapter I want to describe some of the things that have become like glue.

The book of God

Perhaps the most important cohesive factor in our growth as a gathered-and-dispersed church has been the Bible, the Word of God. We have always been a Bible-based church at St Andrew's. Since my arrival in January 1997, we had been very clear and uncompromising about the importance of God's Word. We had increased greatly the emphasis on biblical preaching and biblical theology, and in July 2004 we had made a stand for biblical orthodoxy in our diocese of St Albans. The Bible, accordingly, is of inestimable value to us as a church. Indeed, there can be no revival without a tremendous hunger for the Word of God. As John Wesley once said, 'I am a creature of a day, passing through life as an arrow through the air. A few moments hence, I am no more seen – I drop into eternity. I want to know one thing – the way to Heaven. God has given us a way, written in the Good Book, the Bible. O, give me that book! At any price, give me the Book of God!'

One of the things we decided when we left the building in January 2005 was that I would take on a 'servant leadership' role in my capacity as the vicar of the church. That new role consisted of writing materials for all the MSC leadership teams. At the centre we would decide the theme and the Bible passages for the following term's preaching in the MSCs and I would then spend hours and hours alone with the Lord preparing the notes for all the MSCs for that following term.

The first series we developed was entitled 'Six Months of Purpose' and was drawn up in the autumn of 2004, in preparation for the exodus from the building at the time of the refurbishment. We decided that we would take Rick Warren's book *The Purpose Driven Life* and create a six-month series out of it. Warren had clearly identified the five main purposes of the Christian life as the following:

WORSHIP: You were planned for God's pleasure.
COMMUNITY: You were formed for God's family.
DISCIPLESHIP: You were created to become like Christ.
SERVICE: You were shaped for serving God.
MISSION: You were made for a mission.

This was a great place for the MSCs to start. We all felt that these fivefold purposes were very useful tools for the MSCs to create their own sense of identity and destiny. At the same time, I wanted to make sure all the materials were rooted and grounded properly in the Word of God. I didn't want the people tasked with teaching in the MSCs simply to base their ideas on their own experience. I was determined that every principle would be explored in relation to a Bible passage. With that in mind, I felt led by the Holy Spirit to create a six-month series based in the book of Ephesians. That way each MSC would not only become more purposeful, but would also dig deep into a book of the Bible.

In the end, we looked at the following each month of the first six months of 2005:

> January: Purpose: Created for a Reason
> February: Purpose 1: Planned for God's Pleasure (Worship)
> March: Purpose 2: Formed for God's Family (Community)
> April: Purpose 3: Conformed to Christ's Likeness (Discipleship)
> May: Purpose 4: Shaped for God's Service (Service)
> June: Purpose 5: Called to God's Mission Field (Mission)

In each month we provided enough material for three Sundays and we explored each of the subjects in relation to a passage in Ephesians. This led to the following breakdown:

JANUARY (PURPOSE)
God's Purpose for His People (Eph. 1:1–8)
The Plan Behind the Passion (Eph. 2:14–18)
We Know What the Future Holds! (Eph. 1:9–14)

FEBRUARY (WORSHIP)
Expressing Your Love for the Father (Eph. 3:14–21)
Giving the Son the Highest Honour (Eph. 1:15–23)
Keeping Plugged in to the Holy Spirit (Eph. 5:15–20)

MARCH (COMMUNITY)
God's House, God's Family (Eph. 2:19–22)
Every Person has a Part to Play (Eph. 4:1–16)

APRIL (DISCIPLESHIP)
Learning to Be Like Jesus (Eph. 5:1–14)
Learning to Talk Like Jesus (Eph. 4:17–32)
Learning to Walk Like Jesus (Eph. 5:15–6:9)

MAY (SERVICE)
Every Believer is a Masterpiece (Eph. 2:1–10)
Every Believer has a Mission from God (Eph. 3:1–7)
Every Believer has a God-given Shape (Eph. 4:4–13)

JUNE (MISSION)
Discovering God's Calling for your Life (Eph. 4:1–3)
Rejoicing in your Unique Life Mission (Eph. 3:8–13)
Overcoming the Enemy's Opposition (Eph. 6:10–20)

This practice has continued since we moved back into the building in the autumn of 2005. The only difference is that the series developed for the MSCs are preached at the centre as well as in the MSCs. This has led to greater cohesion as we have looked together at the same subjects and passages throughout the whole expanding network of St Andrew's Church.

In this great challenge, every MSC is supposed to find creative ways of communicating biblical truths to its members. I made three rules in a meeting with the MSC leaders on 2 February 2005. I told them they were not to imitate 'big church' preaching models. In other words, 'passive learning' was to be discouraged. Those entrusted with the privilege of teaching God's Word were not to give a thirty-minute sermon with everyone else listening. Rather they were to be

INNOVATIVE
INVOLVING
INTERACTIVE

And so they have been! Every MSC has found creative, participatory and dialogical models of teaching the Word of God. Indeed, it has been a joy to see the creativity of God's people as they have tailored the ministry of the Word of God to their specific mission contexts. Today, St Andrew's Church is not taught by a few ordained 'experts' at the front of a church building; it is taught by over one hundred anointed, hidden communicators – ordinary people doing extraordinary things for God. It is not taught in one place but in many diverse places. It isn't just taught to those who can read and write but to those who can't. It isn't just taught to those who have big houses but to those who have no home at all. It isn't just taught to those who can hear but to those who are deaf, in sign language. Doesn't that sound like the Kingdom of God to you?

Fourth and fifth Sundays

Our decision right at the start of this great adventure to have all our MSCs come back into the centre on every fourth Sunday for a celebration and to use fifth Sundays for refreshment and resourcing has been a major and much-needed source of cohesion as we have seen more and more of the spontaneous expansion of the church.

The fourth Sundays have given us two great gifts. They have first of all enabled us to baptise new believers at the centre. When people come to Christ through the many outreach activities conducted by MSCs, they are brought back to the centre to share their testimony and then be baptised by full immersion. During the vacancy from July 1996 to 18 January 1997 (after David Pytches retired and before I was inducted as the new vicar) the church had installed a baptistery at the front of St Andrew's Church. They had done so as an act of faith that in the future there would be a great need for a place where first-time converts could be totally immersed in the waters of baptism. I am so proud of the people of that era for having that kind of foresight and courage, because it was 'for such a time as this'. After we returned to the building in the autumn of 2005 we had nearly thirty baptisms at the fourth-Sunday evening central celebrations over the following nine months. The testimonies we heard brought tears of joy to many eyes, especially the stories of those who came to Christ through the outreach of our youth leader Pete Wynter and his team, not to mention the members of Haven MSC, who have worked tirelessly among the homeless and the severely addicted. It is no exaggeration to say that there are some folk in heaven because of Haven's compassionate mission to the marginalised.

The second gift the fourth Sundays gave us was the opportunity for me to recast the vision to everyone. One thing I had learned over the years was the importance of the senior leader using the pulpit to keep the vision alive. We have been very acutely conscious of how risky this whole MSC venture is but we have also sensed a strong calling to step out in faith, and that faith comes by hearing. In overseeing this growing organism, the pulpit has assumed a vital importance for us, especially on the fourth Sundays. It has been the place from which the new apostolic ethos of St Andrew's Church has been constantly strengthened.

On every fourth Sunday I have found new ways of communicating this apostolic ethos. It can be encapsulated in two quotations. The first is from the last words of Jesus to his team before the Ascension. In Matthew 28:18–20 we read:

> *Then Jesus came to them and said, 'All authority in heaven and on earth has been given to me. Therefore go and make disciples of all nations, baptising them in the name of the Father and of the Son and of the Holy Spirit, and teaching them to obey everything I have commanded you. And surely I am with you always, to the very end of the age.'*

Time and again I have stressed that the calling of the church is not to stay behind the four walls of a stone building but to break out into all the world and make disciples. This is our PURPOSE, and the mission-shaped vision has been at the heart of all we have tried to do at St Andrew's in the last five years or so. We are a PURPOSE-FILLED community and we are a PRESENCE-SHAPED community. Jesus told us to go, but he also promised his presence as we go: 'Surely I am with you always, to the very end of the age.'

This brings me to the second quotation. If the first is from Jesus, the second is from Michael Frost and Alan Hirsch. The one book I found really inspiring and helpful in the key stage of risk between 2004 and 2005 was *The Shaping of Things to Come*. I had read this book twice – one of the very rare times in my life I have done that. Both times it clarified what we were called to be and do as a church. In fact, it broke a sense of isolation for me personally because it enabled me to see that we were not alone in this courageous undertaking, that the Holy Spirit was stirring other leaders into radical, apostolic mode all over the world. Here is one of many purple passages from that volume: 'The Come-to-Us stance taken by the attractional church is unbiblical. It's not found in the Gospels or the Epistles. Jesus, Paul, the disciples, the early church leaders all had a Go-to-Them mentality.'

When I read that, I realised we were not alone and that this was the essence that Drew and I were called jealously and fearlessly to guard. Quotations like these helped to awaken the apostolic imagination throughout the whole church. Various key catchphrases have also been important, such as 'putting the adventure back into the Christian venture', 'we are called to be risk-takers, not undertakers', and 'one touch from the King changes everything'. These have all played their part. But teaching the biblical basis for our vision on the fourth and fifth Sundays has been an indispensable means of keeping the glue strong. We have learned to appreciate the importance of the large gathering or celebration for keeping on message.

The importance of latte

In keeping a strong sense of cohesion another key factor has been the training of our MSC leaders. When we moved back into the building in the autumn of 2005 I announced that we would be beginning a course entitled Latte. It is well known throughout St Andrew's that I love good coffee and cannot stand bad, church coffee. I am on record as saying that I believe serving great church coffee is one of the keys to revival! It was perhaps with that in mind that I came up with an acronym for our leadership training course:

L = Leadership
A = And
T = Theology
T = Training
E = Evenings

The first Latte course was held in the autumn of 2005 on Wednesday evenings (with one all-day Saturday intensive per term) and has been running every term since. Latte is a course designed to equip our MSC leadership teams with sound biblical theology and also the tools they need for leading effectively in mission. This is a really important part of our calling at the centre. Everything stands or falls on the quality of the leaders that are sent out from the centre to influence groups of people in mission. If the leaders are ill-equipped, or if their theological foundations are weak, then the whole work can implode. Having been a curate at St Thomas' Crookes at the time when the famous Nine O'Clock Service began to go off the rails, I had made an inner vow never to let leaders become unaccountable in any venture I was called to oversee – hence Latte.

One reason why Latte has been important is because most MSC leaders have felt the need to learn 'on the go'. Rather than spending three years learning in a theological college and then being sent out on mission, these leaders have been sent out on mission and then learned theology. This is a point well made by Frost and Hirsch: 'Some critics of the missional church ask, "Where is the Bible taught? How do people learn doctrine?" We recognise these as valid questions. But we believe such learning takes place more effectively when the Christian faith community is involved in active mission . . . like Jesus' first followers discovered, learning occurs when we need to draw on information because a situation demands it.'

This is precisely what we have discovered. So I have so far composed courses on subjects such as Christian Doctrine (which is now available in my book, *The User's Guide to Christian Belief*), John's Gospel, Luke: Acts and Mission, Lessons in Twenty-first-century Leadership, Pauline Literature, Bible and Church History overview, Evangelism in a Postmodern Age, School of Apologetics, and so on. These have been geared to the needs of MSC leaders in particular.

A leadership mosaic

Perhaps the most important course I've developed is 'The Leadership Mosaic'. During a period of study leave (January to April 2007) I set myself the task of finding a top-quality training course for pioneer leaders. I looked everywhere for something that would be useful to us before realising yet again that I was being called to write it myself. On the thirteen-hour flight back from Singapore to Heathrow in January 2007 I started to compose a leadership training course based on the life of Moses as told in the book of Exodus. As I did so, I began thinking around the idea of a Leadership Mosaic (next page), a patterned design based around Moses' story.

At the heart of Moses' leadership was intimate 'communion' with God, his face-to-face friendship with the Lord. This is the core of all spiritual leadership.

Out of that relationship came a calling to become a pioneering leader who would take God's people from a restrictive reality into a new and spacious place.

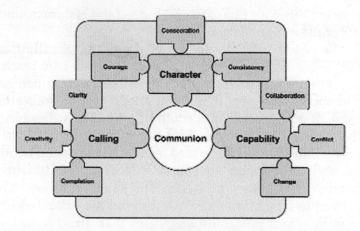

In relation to this calling, Moses would have a great clarity and consistency about his priorities, he would call forth extraordinary creativity from God's people, and he would reach the completion of the task by bringing his followers to the very edge of the Promised Land.

In developing as a leader, the issue of character was vital. Moses had to learn to manage his anger and he learned in the wilderness, in the desert school of leadership. Throughout his life, Moses exhibited strong character traits, such as courage in facing Pharaoh, consistency by not being a crowd-pleaser, and consecration to God's high standards of holiness (classically expressed in the Ten Commandments).

As Moses grew, he cultivated certain essential leadership capabilities. Some of the most visible concerned collaboration (dispersing leadership throughout his organisation by decentralising power and control), as well as managing conflict and change. That Moses developed these capabilities is evident in his communicational ability. At the time of his calling (Exodus 3–4) Moses complains that he is a poor speaker. Yet by the time we reach Exodus 15 Moses has communicated very clearly with both Pharaoh and indeed the Hebrews, and the stutterer is even singing!

The Leadership Mosaic is a vital part of our calling at the centre. At the same time I do stress when I am teaching it that it is not exhaustive. The Mosaic is fragmented and incomplete and it is the trainees' responsibility to think of other words that could be added to it. Teaching this course has been one of the most rewarding experiences of my life as I have seen leaders in formation being visibly transformed into more effective and dynamic twenty-first-century pioneers. The story of Moses has proved to be extremely relevant to our situation, which is more about portable tabernacles than fixed temples. At the beginning of the Leadership Mosaic course we quote John McKay (Whitby Conference, 1947): 'The whole church must . . . become a mobile missionary force, ready for a wilderness life . . . It is time for us all to be thinking of campaign tents rather than of cathedrals.' Amen to that!

I cannot emphasise strongly enough the importance of spending quality time resourcing leaders in mission. Drew and I have invested a great deal of time in this. Drew's focus has been on the midweek 'huddles' that he and the MSC staff (David and Jenny Rosser and Ruth May) have regularly been holding with MSC leaders. The huddle idea is something that Drew borrowed from St Thomas' Crookes and it has been a vital part of keeping the glue strong. During these evening meetings with MSC leadership teams Drew and his staff support team are able to keep their ears very close to the ground and bring quality support to those on the front line of our church's mission.

These 'huddle' meetings happen every term in the homes of MSC leaders. Drew asks how the leaders are getting on personally and spiritually. In addition, he enquires what the Holy Spirit has been saying to them as a leadership team and how they are acting on that. The huddles end with Drew and the staff laying hands on the leaders and praying for them. Often prophetic words of encouragement are shared. These huddles have been invaluable for strengthening the relational bond between the MSC leaders and the senior staff of St Andrew's.

In addition to these huddle meetings, Drew and his MSC departmental staff have been focused on weekly emails and telephone calls with the MSC leaders. Of particular importance have been Drew's weekly Mini-bites in which he shares a thought for the week (often a quotation about pioneering mission) and in which there is an opportunity for each MSC to write back with a testimony about what the Lord has done the previous weekend. Testimonies have always been vital in the journey we have undertaken. They are shared widely as a means of ensuring 'best practice exchange'. John Wimber used to say, 'Celebrate what you want to propagate,' and we have certainly done that in the last five years – not least through 'the Gold Index', a termly magazine published by the MSC department and given to everyone in the church.

Another focus for Drew has been promoting great testimonies through visual media. To help in this we pushed for the appointment of a visual media consultant and happily the PCC agreed. Caz Puntis came to us with a great track record in TV and media in February 2007 and has worked with the MSC department in creating media to serve the MSC strategy. Her superb DVD presentation of the MSC leaders' weekend away in 2007 was shown to the whole church several weeks later on one of our fourth-Sunday gatherings. This, as with all Caz's work, has brought greater cohesion, clarity and unity to the whole operation.

While Drew's focus has been on huddles, Mini-bites and visual media, my focus has been on Latte and the sessions I have with all the MSC leaders every fifth Sunday. During these fifth-Sunday sessions I am able to listen to the MSC leaders as well as equip and encourage them in the amazing work they're doing. These are often times of refocusing, like the session (February 2006) in which I underlined the importance of the MSCs embracing the three Ms:

MISSION
MIRACLES
MULTIPLICATION

When I taught into those three concepts I was reminding the MSC leaders that their task is to reach out to the lost (not just build a strong sense of Christian community), to pray for signs and wonders, and to multiply when they reach fifty adults. This was an example of the kind of realignment that happens when we meet with our leaders – a realignment that keeps everyone singing from the same song sheet and moving in the same direction.

Finding strong symbols

One of the most important tasks in keeping us all together has been the use of striking stories and symbols that bring clarity to our mission. One of the strongest of these has been the idea of St Andrew's as a lifeboat church. This is a dream I came to St Andrew's with in 1996–97. I had told the PCC in November 1996 that St Andrew's was to become a place from which many lifeboats were launched. On the fourth Sunday of 2006 (almost exactly ten years later) I told the church that we now had many lifeboats, some inshore and some off-shore, that were rescuing those in peril on the sea of life. During that talk I drew attention to a number of parallels between the lifeboat service and the new St Andrew's. I particularly emphasised the importance of everyone being committed to one single purpose, saving lives, and everyone having a vital role to play, whether at the lifeboat station (the centre) or out at sea in the lifeboats (the MSCs). I made one particular point about togetherness, saying, 'In a lifeboat station, you don't have a situation where the people working there say after a launch, "Thank goodness the lifeboat has gone. All they ever talk about here is lifeboats!" Nor do you have a situation where the lifeboat crew, after putting out to sea, says, "Thank goodness we've left that lot behind. Let's go on a booze cruise to France!" Instead, everyone is valued. Everyone is committed to the task of "saving those at sea" (the RNLI mission statement). So it is with us. There is no divide between those in MSCs and those based at the centre. We are all of us "Partners in Rescue".'

Finding strong analogies like this is very important for cohesion. This is especially true of volunteer-intensive organisations like churches. In such communities you cannot appeal to contracts and salaries to motivate allegiance. As in the RNLI, very few people are paid; the vast majority of the workers are volunteers. You therefore have to find far more creative means of motivation. The lifeboat analogy has been especially unifying in our situation. It has helped us understand that we are here to continue Jesus' ministry of rescue and it has helped to foster a sense of shared purpose. It has helped to create a volunteer spirit and combat consumerism.

The lifeboat symbol has therefore been an example of the Holy Spirit giving us pictures that can fuel the fire of mission. Indeed, I have had some remarkable confirmations that this has been the Lord's gift to us. When I went on study leave in January 2007, my first port of call was Sydney, Australia. I visited a few mega-churches that I had had in mind to see in action. But it was not in those but in a very small, mission-shaped church that I found most inspiration. There I met a pastor called Paul who asked me what was happening in St Andrew's and I shared the story of our transition from cruise liner to lifeboat station. He was visibly excited and then asked whether I was aware of the brand new evangelism training course by Reinhard Bonnke. I said no. He then showed me a DVD that Reinhard's organisation has put a lot of investment into called *Lost at Sea*. It was a short movie (with excellent production qualities) of a cruise liner called *Corpus Christi* ('the Body of Christ') that was mandated by the coastguard to rescue the survivors of another ship that had just sunk nearby. Even though the *Corpus Christi* had more than sixty lifeboats, it launched only a handful because the people on board wanted to have a church service instead.

When I saw this movie I was deeply moved. The first opportunity I had on returning from my study leave in April 2007 I showed *Lost at Sea* to all the MSC leaders in my session with them on the fifth Sunday of that month. They were deeply stirred. Many of them reacted the same way I had when I saw it in Sydney. We were pretty well all of us convicted, and a dramatic refocusing on mission took place that morning in the MSCs. One of the MSC leaders, Trevor Jenkins, wrote this email to me:

> On Sunday after the Rest and Resource sessions I drove home. As I turned onto Stag Lane there was a car in front

of me. The driver wasn't that brilliant. Argh! He turned down Shepherds Lane, so I had to follow him for even longer. His driving became even more erratic. If only I could pass him and get away: the road rage began to build.

Then God spoke: 'Look at the back window.' Oh yeah, there's an RNLI sticker. 'No, really: look.' Oh, it says, 'Blah, blah, blah, lifeboats.' 'NO, REALLY LOOK.' By this time I can see that the sticker says, 'Support blah Lifeboats', but I can't quite make out the second word.

By the time we get to the Shepherd School and the speed bumps I'm very nearly sitting on the back seat of this car, the driver was going sooooo slowwww.

'LOOK!'

Oh, ah: it says, 'Support our Lifeboats.'

A second confirmation of the rightness of this analogy came on that same Sunday morning when I showed *Lost at Sea* with the MSC leaders. One of the MSC leaders attending that morning – Hugh Lloyd – had just been rescued by a lifeboat several weeks before that! This was his story:

We were on a working holiday at our cottage in Pembrokeshire and I was going to get a morning paper and take Tigga for a walk at about 8.00 am. The shop selling papers had just moved about six hundred yards so I was not on my old route. I was taking Tigga in a field (next to the coast path) which I thought was totally fenced. I just turned a corner and saw a gap in the fence where a gate was missing. I thought I should put Tigga on the lead, when she spotted a rabbit, was off through the gap onto the coast path and to my dismay straight over the cliff. This is about 150 feet high at this point. With my heart in my mouth I rushed round the headland saw the tide was in, praise the Lord, and Tigga was swimming out to an island. She got onto a small ledge and I could see she was badly cut and shivering.

I gave thanks that she was alive and in an adrenalin rush somehow got down the cliff-face, which is pretty sheer, in one piece, and was opposite her, about twenty yards away. I called to her but she was too scared to swim back, and after about twenty minutes I realised we needed help. I called out for about twenty minutes but there was no response. It was windy, and being at the bottom of the cliff meant it would be very hard for anyone to hear me, especially with very few people around so early in the morning.

I then prayed for help and within two minutes the wind dropped and two Danish hikers heard me. They had a mobile phone (with a signal, even though most mobiles do not work in the area) and called the coastguard, who then arrived, said help was on the way, and in turn called the lifeboat station at St Davids. We were rescued (me first, as Tigga would not move) by the inshore lifeboat (with a four-man crew) about forty minutes later and taken to Solva harbour. The coastguard called ahead to Pat, who met me, and we took Tigga to the vet, who had heat pads and painkillers at the ready. Later that afternoon they operated and sewed her up. She has made a remarkable recovery.

A third striking confirmation happened a few weeks later when I was speaking in Dudley at a Revival Fires conference for Trevor and Sharon Baker. In the speakers' lounge I met a man called Rick Oldland. Rick is a missiologist who leads Ansdell Baptist Church and lectures on church planting all over the world on behalf of Partners in Harvest. He had heard me speaking about the lifeboat model of church and came up to me and introduced himself. He shared that he was not only a church leader and an itinerant missiologist but also a member of the lifeboat crew at Lytham St Anne's! Here was someone who understood first-hand the strong analogy between saving those at sea and saving those in peril on the sea of life. Within six months Rick had come to one of our fourth-Sunday gatherings and spoken to the whole church about the similarities between the lifeboat service and the church's mission.

Strong analogies (vocalised in symbol and story) are vital for cohesion. No analogy is perfect, of course, and it is only fair to say that we have had one or two people pick holes in the details of the lifeboat picture. No analogy is permanent either. While the lifeboat analogy has served us very well over time, there is no suggestion that this will remain the dominant cohesive image in the coming season. Every analogy may well have a shelf-life. It is up to the leaders to discern when the analogy has lost its power to excite and has started to irritate rather than motivate God's people. Then the task is to find a new analogy that can ignite the prophetic imagination of God's people.

Creating a virtuoso team

In my case, I am under no illusions about the fact that I am very blessed to be surrounded by a highly creative team of people. I do not have to think these things up all on my own. I have a group of extremely gifted people in the staff team of St Andrew's who stimulate endless amounts of creative and imaginative thought. They are the best bunch of people I have ever worked with and there is no doubt that St Andrew's would never have achieved the levels of growth we have witnessed

without their invaluable contribution. It is the staff team
that has helped to create the cohesion I have been speaking about in this chapter. Having a united staff team has
created a ripple effect throughout the whole network of
St Andrew's Church. They are the ones who have
resourced the amazing work of the 150 or so MSC leaders on the front line of pioneering mission in our local-
ity. From a strongly united team working at the centre of
St Andrew's, the mission of God has spread like wildfire
locally, regionally, nationally and – increasingly – globally.

One of the people I quote a lot is Frances Hesselbein.
She was responsible for turning the North American Girl
Scouts organisation from an ailing to a thriving institution. She did this by employing what she calls a 'circular'
model of leadership. Instead of operating a hierarchical,
triangular model, she decided to decentralise leadership
and engage in strategic collaboration:

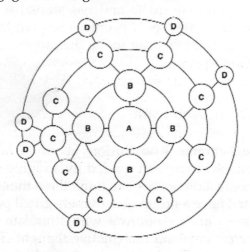

A President/CEO
B Vice President(s)
C Group Directors
D Team Directors

This is in fact what a lot of leadership philosophers are encouraging today. They talk about the importance of inverting pyramids and of choosing circular models in which leadership is dispersed throughout an organisation rather than held in the hands of a few. Moses learned this more than three millennia ago when Jethro came and told him that he was doing too much and needed to delegate to leaders of tens, fifties, hundreds and thousands (Exodus 18). We have had to learn this lesson as well.

Margaret Wheatley talks powerfully about this change in the understanding of leadership in her seminal book *Leadership and the New Science*. She speaks eloquently about the change from a Newtonian, mechanistic worldview to the new worldview of quantum physics. This is a change from a world based on machine images with boundaries (where everyone knows their place) to a world based on fluid images to do with waves, relationships and the vast web of life. In such a time of change, 'The era of the rugged individual has been replaced by the era of the team player.' Here, power is generated through relationships. The quality of these relationships is what makes an organisation effective and – to quote Margaret Wheatley – 'Love is the most potent source of power.' This is why we live in a world where small groups of highly motivated people can change the politics of the most powerful nations on earth.

At St Andrew's I have been very blessed to have a united and very loving team. In fact, I am surrounded by self-starters – highly motivated, low-maintenance leaders. I could not ask for a more capable right-hand man than Drew Williams and I know he couldn't have asked for more able staff than David and Jenny Rosser and the ever-ebullient Ruth May. We would never have seen the mobilisation of an army of minstrels without the leadership of our worship director Belinda Patrick, who for me represents the best of the best. We would never have been able to resource the children's groups in some of our MSCs without the amazing work of our children's leaders Dave and Julie Hill (and latterly Andy Hayball) and Louise Dyer. We would never have seen so many lives changed without the expert and loving leadership of John and Heather Cowan, who have overseen the development of prayer ministry throughout the network. We would never have seen the advances locally and beyond without the prayer cover provided by Helen Clark and her passionate intercession team. This is just to name a few of the unsung heroes of the work. I could mention the outstanding church wardens I have had lifting up my arms, as Aaron and Hur did for Moses – particularly Peter Doyle and Mike Cooke. I could mention Caz Puntis and Oli Griffiths, who run our visual media department, and Pete Wynter, our youth pastor, whose teens have in many ways led the way. I could mention all the interns we have had helping us in our mission over the last three years. I could mention the administration department – those overseeing our finances (Brian Plumridge and Arthur Taverner) and the church office (Alan Pledger, Judith Davies, Natasha Taylor, and Joanna Appel, and my present, invaluable PA Tiff Vale). I could mention others who have been on my clergy team in the last four or five years – Nicky Pledger, Jim Sutton and Greg Downes, to name just three.

There is no doubt in my heart that it is the quality of the team at the centre that has been responsible in no small way for the unity and the creativity of the work here in recent years. Marc Dupont – a prophet now based in Dayton, Ohio – visited St Andrew's Church right at the beginning of my time as vicar. In 1997 he ministered to the staff team as it was then and told us all, 'When the team is in place, revival will come.' That word was for ten years later. Today we are enjoying a season of unprecedented fruitfulness at St Andrew's and it is the team who must take so much credit for that. From a united and loving core team, the ripples of well-being have spread outwards to the furthest reaches of our mission. I therefore cannot stress the importance of having a virtuoso team. As Jim Collins says, 'If we spend the vast majority of our time with people we love and respect – people we really enjoy being on the bus with and who will never disappoint us – then we will almost certainly have a great life, no matter where the bus goes.' That is my story.

The St Andrew's experience

A final factor in terms of cohesion has been a strong sense of unity about who we are and where we are heading. The staff team at the centre, in partnership with the MSC leadership teams and our PCC, have been absolutely critical in keeping a sense of focus on these issues over the last five years. It is with these teams that I have talked about identity and destiny, seeking to keep the vision fresh and alive in the corporate memory of our people as we move ahead through uncharted terrain.

In Chapter 1 I mentioned Mike Breen's 'four Vs' (diagram next page).

As we have travelled together as a church, we have had to return to these four Vs and grow sharper in our focus in every case. The first V, Vision, has become clearer. We have always had an emphasis on taking the Father's love out into a lost world. But in 2007 we became even more sharply focused in the statement of our vision. Now it reads as follows: 'Our dream at St Andrew's Church is to bring the Father's love to the fatherless, especially through extended families.'

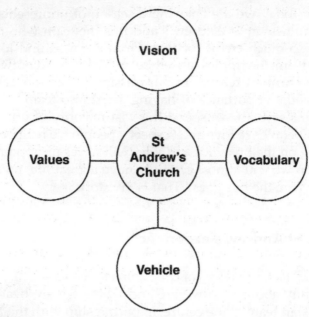

'Extended families' brings me to the second V, Vehicle. We are now an MSC church and MSCs are our primary vehicle for spreading the Father's love to a world in great need. In 2007 we have sharpened up on the MSC shape. Following Jethro's advice to Moses in Exodus 18, we now stress that fifty is the maximum number of adults in an MSC and that the leaders need to start planning for multiplication when they reach thirty-five. These numbers keep each MSC from losing its mission and multiplication focus.

The third V we have had to refine is Values. When I was on my study leave at the beginning of 2007, I read a book called *The Starbucks Experience*. I am a fan of great coffee, especially Starbucks, so this was not a hard book to read, nor was Howard Schultz's *Pour Your Heart into It*. Schultz is the CEO of Starbucks and has described himself unashamedly as 'a coffee evangelist'. In taking

his coffee to the world, Schultz has stressed the importance of 'staying small while growing big' – exactly what
we have been seeing at St Andrew's. He also stressed the
important role of the baristas, the people in every coffee
shop behind the counter who relate to those who come
into these small communities of coffee drinkers. The
baristas are the equivalent of our MSC leaders. The
Starbucks coffee shops have for Schultz been designed
as a 'third place' – a place that people prioritise after
home and work for gathering to socialise. This again is
similar to what we have been trying to do with the
MSCs, establishing a meaningful alternative community
for lonely postmodern people. So we have much in
common with Starbucks.

The thing I found most challenging of all was
Schultz's emphasis on what he called 'the Starbucks
Experience'. Schultz had defined the core values that
made up the Starbucks Experience and which he expected to see replicated and exhibited in every Starbucks
coffee shop throughout the world. These five values
were:

- Make it your Own
- Everything Matters
- Surprise and Delight
- Embrace Resistance
- Leave your Mark

Reading this led me to ask a vital question. What is 'The
St Andrew's Experience'? What are the values that we
hold dear as a church and which I expect to see replicated and exhibited in every one of our MSCs, and indeed
at the centre? This led me to a time of revisiting our values with the staff team and the MSC leadership teams. In
the end we came up with the following statement:

ST ANDREW'S VALUES

Staying small while growing big

We are a church of the Word and the Spirit, seeking to bring the Father's love to the fatherless, especially through extended families. In all of this, we highly cherish the following values:

- Pursuing God's Presence
- Biblical Truth
- Everyone Matters
- Keeping it Real
- Authentic Community
- Releasing Everyone to Fulfil their Potential
- Reaching the Lost

This is 'The St Andrew's Experience', and we expect to see this exhibited throughout every expression of community in our network of congregations, mid-sized communities and churches.

The fourth and final V we looked at again was Vocabulary. Embarking on the MSC strategy had led to a whole new set of concepts. The most important has been the idea of an MSC, a Mid-Sized Community. While everyone agreed that this abbreviation described exactly what an MSC is, Drew and I felt that it was also a bit bland. With that in mind we decided to keep the letters 'MSC' and change the meaning from Mid-Sized Community to Mission-Shaped Community. This has helped us once again to keep a sharp sense of focus and to reinforce the glue that binds us all together in an organisation where the entrepreneurial spirit is increasingly evident.

Some unfinished business

In the final analysis, what has held us all together in this gathered-and-dispersed model of church is the work of the Holy Spirit. No one should be under any illusions about the one primarily responsible for the adventure that St Andrew's has been enjoying in recent years. This is the work of the Holy Spirit, who has joined hearts together in a vital and energising way. St Andrew's Church is not a building, it is a people, and it is a people with hearts filled by the one Holy Spirit. St Andrew's makes a big crowd, but far more important than the crowd is the cloud – the cloud of the Spirit of God – which has moved us on from where we were in 1997 to a whole new reality. The cloud has moved and so have we. Only a tiny number have gone elsewhere. Only a very small fraction of our people have moaned, lamented and criticised. The vast majority have said, 'Yes, we will follow the cloud,' and in the process hundreds and hundreds of people have been set free from a place of restriction to a broad and spacious place in which they can truly use their gifts. It has been thrilling to watch the ministry of the Spirit in recent years. We know it is him and we give glory to the Father through the Son for his mighty recalibration of the church.

What is it that the Holy Spirit has been doing among us at St Andrew's? George Barna would use the word 'Revolution'. That is the title of a controversial book of his, in which he says this: 'Rather than relying on a relative handful of inspired preachers to promote a national revival, the emerging Revolution is truly a grassroots explosion of commitment to God that will refine the Church and result in a natural and widespread immersion in outreach.' Revolution is one possibility. Another is the word 'Reformation'. This is a word I have used with our MSC leaders, particularly in a presentation I gave to them in 2006 on 'Finishing what the Reformers Started'. There I spoke of living in a generation in which we had the opportunity to complete what people like Martin Luther had started. Luther had talked a lot about the priesthood of believers, and yet Protestant denominations ended up being as priest-ridden as the church they had originally protested against. I quoted Greg Ogden: 'There is a fresh wind blowing in the church today that is being felt wherever the doors are thrown open to include all of God's people in ministry. We live in a day of a paradigm shift.' I believed that then; I believe it even more today.

What is in no doubt to many of us is that the Holy Spirit is working powerfully among us as a church, as in our history before. We are in a season in which new wine is being poured into a new wineskin. The model we have been led to use at St Andrew's is just one of these new wineskins. It is not the only one, because the Holy Spirit is more creative than that. He does not use a 'one-size-fits-all' approach. At the same time, it is the Holy Spirit who has given us the lead and kept us together on the incredible journey that we've been on. If this is a completion of the Reformation, or indeed the beginning of a Second Reformation, then all I can say is, 'Bring it on, Lord!' And let all the glory go to Jesus!

9

RUMOURS OF REFORMATION

Andrew Williams

1516

In 1516 a Dominican friar named Johann Tetzel was sent to Germany on the orders of the Pope, Leo X, to raise money to rebuild St Peter's Basilica in Rome. The building site in Rome was a 'Who's Who' of architects and sculptors, with Michelangelo rubbing shoulders with Da Vinci and a whole host of Italian Renaissance 'luvvies'. Their artistic endeavours, together with Leo X's liking for wild parties, had bled the Vatican coffers dry.

The papacy hit upon a winning money-making strategy, fresh from Leo X's Treasure House of Merit – you could indulge yourself. With a little paper scroll bearing the papal seal – for a sum of money – you could buy yourself some forgiveness. They even had a catchy jingle: 'As soon as the coin in the coffer rings, the soul from purgatory springs.' Thirty years later the papal campaign buses rolled into a little windswept corner of Germany called Wittenberg. That same night, in a small display of polite disagreement, an unknown parish priest nailed a copy of his theses to the door of

Wittenberg parish church – church doors in those days acting as a kind of blogging site.

The ideas that were nailed to the door that night included the scandalous notions that faith could not be mediated by the church but that salvation was attainable by faith in Jesus Christ alone, that the Word of God should be in the language and the hearts of all people, and that contrary to medieval church propaganda that taught that Christians were to be divided into two classes, 'spiritual' and 'temporal', in truth all baptised Christians are 'priests' in the sight of God. The author of these theses immediately became the enemy of the Holy Catholic Church. The unknown German priest was Martin Luther and what was nailed to the door that night let loose a priesthood of all believers that would change the entire course of western civilisation.

1738

On 24 May 1738 at a meeting in Aldersgate Street, London, an unknown Anglican vicar heard a reading of Martin Luther's preface to Paul's letter to the Romans and wrote, 'I felt my heart strangely warmed.' What he received that day revolutionised his ministry. A few weeks later he preached a sermon on the doctrine of salvation by faith, which was followed by another, on God's grace, 'Free in all, and free for all'. From that moment he never stopped preaching the importance of faith for salvation and the witness of God's Spirit within the spirit of the believer that they are truly a child of God. Almost immediately he became an enemy of the Reformed Anglican Church. Overcoming his scruples, in April 1739 he preached his first open-air sermon near

Bristol. He continued for fifty years – entering churches when he was invited and preaching the Gospel in fields, halls, cottages and chapels, when Anglican churches closed their doors to him.

He was persecuted by the authorities, including his ordained colleagues. He was attacked in sermons and in print and at times assaulted by mobs. He and his followers were denounced as heretics, and some claimed that they were trying to re-establish Catholicism. Undaunted, he remained at work among the poor and encouraged the release of the priesthood of all believers to lead, to preach and to love God's people. On Wednesday 2 March, 1791, in his eighty-eighth year, John Wesley died peacefully, leaving as the result of his life's work more than one hundred thousand Spirit-filled Christians, and over five hundred itinerant preachers under the name 'Methodist'.

1906

Just over a hundred years later, the one-eyed son of a former slave was receiving tuition from a Methodist-trained minister in Topeka, Kansas. Because this student was black, he was seated outside the classroom, in the hall, segregated from the white students. From his place in the hall his heart was strangely warmed. In spring 1906 this student was invited to speak in a black Nazarene church in Los Angeles, where he preached that it really had been the Lord's intention to pour out his Spirit on all people – even the poor, black ones. He was locked out of the church. Not to be perturbed, he continued to speak to the poor on front porches and in any home that would receive him. Interest swelled and an abandoned warehouse at 312

Azusa Street was commandeered. The *Los Angeles Times* report of 18 April 1906 takes up the story: 'Coloured people and a sprinkling of whites compose the congregation, and night is made hideous in the neighbourhood by the howling of the worshippers who spend hours swaying back and forth. . . . They claim to have the gift of tongues and to be able to comprehend the babble.'

This itinerant black preacher was William Joseph Seymour, and on 18 April 1906 he opened the door to a move of God that the *Los Angeles Times* could never have imagined. That movement placed the Word, the Spirit and the mission of the church into the hands of a poor, multiracial people who immediately became the enemy of the reformed church – or as it was affectionately known in Azusa Street, 'The Holy Refrigerator'. From these beginnings the Pentecostal church increased steadily throughout the world, until by 1991 it had taken its place as the largest family of Protestant denominations in the world. In January 1999 it was recorded that, around the world, over 450 million people were involved in Pentecostalism, with an annual increase of 19 million per annum. Some 66 per cent of this movement is found in the developing world.

1500 BC

Around 1500 BC a refugee people were brutally taken into slavery by their host country. They were forced to build colossal temples where the ruling family was worshipped. But the more these refugees were oppressed, the more they multiplied. In response, the governing authority worked them ruthlessly – even to death – and in a contemptible and thoroughly evil attempt to control their numbers ordered that every boy-child born to this people should be slaughtered. One unknown baby boy, born to a slave girl, was spared this infanticide by being hidden in a basket beside the river Nile. With great risk to all the parties who conspired in this ridiculous plan, the child was raised as a son of the ruling monarchy, in the bosom of the family that oppressed his people and had slaughtered his peers. The child grew to be a man who would lead his people out of slavery. He immediately became the enemy of the ruling dynasty. At one of the high points in his ministry this leader, Moses, wrote this:

> *Then the cloud covered the Tent of Meeting, and the glory of the LORD filled the tabernacle. Moses could not enter the Tent of Meeting because the cloud had settled upon it, and the glory of the LORD filled the tabernacle. In all the travels of the Israelites, whenever the cloud lifted from above the tabernacle, they would set out; but if the cloud did not lift, they did not set out – until the day it lifted. So the cloud of the LORD was over the tabernacle by day, and fire was in the cloud by night, in the sight of all the house of Israel during all their travels. (Ex. 40:34–38)*

Here is a snapshot in time, when the people of God have actually got it right. In this moment in the history of salvation, under canvas, in the middle of the desert, the people of God are exactly where they should be, having done exactly what was asked of them. And in all his glory, God of the mountain top now enters their campsite.

So in this snapshot, what can we learn? What are the values that the Lord is underscoring by his presence? In this epiphany under canvas there are some godly principles that have undergirded our story.

Tabernacle: the internal aspect

The people of God are tabernacle people. There is an 'inner' and an 'external' aspect to this. Let me deal with the internal part first.

Physically, the tabernacle was just a tent. It was surrounded by a courtyard that was fenced off with curtains but open to the sky. The tent itself was divided into two rooms, the Holy Place and the Most Holy Place. But at this time in the history of salvation the tabernacle was God's earthly address, his royal tent among the tents of Israel.

The tabernacle was designed to teach the people of God who Yahweh is: 'So I will consecrate the Tent of Meeting and the altar and will consecrate Aaron and his sons to serve me as priests. Then I will dwell among the Israelites and be their God. They will know that I am the LORD their God, who brought them out of Egypt' (Ex. 29:44–46).

Never again need they doubt that the Lord their God was with them and for them. This truth was so remarkable that throughout history the people of God could scarcely contain it within their hearts. And across history, every time that truth entered afresh, great things followed.

Following a near-death experience, Martin Luther attempted to make it his life's work to be worthy of God's affection. He disappointed his aspirant natural father. He joined the most severe Augustinian monastic order he could find, he surrendered every human comfort and embarked upon every religious pilgrimage in an attempt to make peace with God. What led Luther to nail his theses to the door of the church in Wittenberg was the unshakeable revelation that because of Jesus, God dwelled within him and he never needed to doubt

that God was with him and for him. The God of the
mountain had moved into the tabernacle of Luther's
heart and the reformation was airborne.

It was the same revelation that came to Wesley as his
heart was 'strangely warmed'. As Wesley lay dying, his
friends gathered around him. It is reported that he
grasped their hands and said repeatedly, 'Farewell,
farewell.' But at the end, summoning all his remaining
strength, he cried out, 'The best of all is, God is with us!'

And in a hallway, outside a 'whites only' classroom, it
was the same revelation that entered the consciousness
of a poor black boy. God of the mountain took residence
in the tabernacle of William Seymour's heart. Seymour's
transformed heart became the marching song of the people of God as the Holy Spirit moved upon the poor and
destitute in downtown Los Angeles. 'O boundless love
divine! How shall this tongue of mine to wondering
mortals tell the matchless grace divine – that I, a child of
hell, should in His image shine! The Comforter has
come!'

To be a people of the tabernacle is to be bearers of this
truth, to hold this revelation within us. To know that
because of the Father's great love, because of Jesus and
what he has done for us on the Cross, by his Holy Spirit,
we are the Lord's earthly residence. His loving presence
is encamped within us.

I think that one of the many powerful contributions
Mark Stibbe has brought to this adventure in his leadership at St Andrew's has been to impart the revelation of
the Father's love. To encourage our MSC leaders and
our people that they are secure in, and serve out of, the
truth that they are loved passionately and uncondition-
ally by the perfect Dad. Because of this, MSCs have
become communities that are suffused with the Father's
love.

This has been a critical factor, because no matter how you come at it, MSCs are a huge personal risk. To belong to an MSC is to take a gamble and to risk finding out whether the Father can really love us through other people. I recall in the early days a registration paper that had been filled out by a church member stating their preference for an MSC. The registration form ended with this request: 'I want to be in an MSC without any muppets!' What we have come to learn is the paradox that a strong MSC is full of muppets. MSCs are communities where imperfect people discover that God is for them; God of the mountain takes residence in the tabernacle of their heart.

Tabernacle: the external aspect

At the end of Exodus, the cloud that had been the guide and 'advance guard' for Israel came to dwell in the Lord's tabernacle. And from that point on, God led his people on their onward journeys: 'In all the travels of the Israelites, whenever the cloud lifted from above the tabernacle, they would set out; but if the cloud did not lift, they did not set out – until the day it lifted. So the cloud of the LORD was over the tabernacle by day, and fire was in the cloud by night, in the sight of all the house of Israel during all their travels' (Ex. 40:36–38).

The rules of engagement were very simple. When God moved, the people moved. The tabernacle was never to contain or constrain God's glory. The tabernacle was to follow wherever God's glory was leading. Our experience over the past four or five years would suggest that nothing has changed the Lord's mind. We remain tabernacle people because our place is always to follow him, to be led by his glory. When the church conspired to tie the presence of God to Rome it might as well have attempted to tie up the wind with string. When the Anglican Church sought to constrain Wesley and his itinerant preachers it made exactly the same mistake. When Seymour moved into a poor neighbourhood in Los Angeles it was because the Lord had already pitched his camp there.

How can we set out whenever the cloud lifts if we have barricaded ourselves in the Temple? From Azusa Street one of Seymour's early Pentecostal preachers declared, 'It is possible to be ever so devout to your church and yet be wrong . . . the true church is not made up of fine buildings, choirs and prima donna singers, nor is it made up of carpeted aisles and cushioned pews.' If we are to be the people to whom God says, 'I will give it to you,' we must be willing and able to pack up our tents and follow after him. At their best; at their most obedient, faithful and free, the people of God were under canvas because so was their God.

As we moved into our fourth year in MSCs the Holy Spirit moved across the network of now more than thirty-two MSCs with renewed inspiration. Suddenly there was a desire to follow after the Holy Spirit and to get out of the community hall or school hall and to go deeper into the neighbourhood.

One MSC that met in Chorleywood was aware that at the end of the street where they met there was a colossal car boot sale, with thousands of people passing through on a Sunday morning. Having spied out the ground, a number of them (aged six to sixty) set up a stand offering free bottles of water to visitors and stallholders. As the team handed out the water, they briefly explained that they were Christians from a nearby church who wanted to show them the Father's love. Many interesting discussions ensued and there were requests for prayer, so much so that the next month they erected an open prayer tent so that they could meet the demand. A similar initiative was happening in Watford, where another MSC went into the local parks handing out bunches of flowers on Mothering Sunday and free cold drinks throughout the summer.

Again sensing the move of the Holy Spirit, another MSC completely refashioned the way they operated on a Sunday. Up until this point they had been meeting in a school dining hall. They had been extremely successful in building bridges with the community but they sensed the Lord's onward call. They turned their Sunday gatherings into a café serving free breakfast to anybody in the community who might like to come. At the start of their Sunday meeting they would meet for thirty minutes to pray and worship together. Then they would divide into three units. One group would go off to prayer-walk the community and to look for God-given opportunities to invite people for breakfast. The second group was in charge of the kitchen and the third welcomed and chatted with visitors. As they had prayed and made their preparations they had asked themselves, will anybody come? But the Lord honoured their faithfulness. There have been many visitors who now make this a part of their Sunday, including a group of young people working in the village as part of their community service orders. Again, perhaps not everybody's favourite child in the community was now sitting down to a good breakfast with the Lord's people.

Haven MSC, drawing alongside the homeless in Watford, had been very fruitful but a sense of the Lord's onward call caused them to reflect and pray. Their evening meetings were a relaxed and loving environment where people had come to know the Lord, but they knew that there were many more on the streets who were not being reached with the Father's love. They set about a new plan, according to which some of their members were assigned to go into the parks of Watford on Sunday morning and invite those who had been sleeping rough to breakfast. In a nearby hall, the rest of the team fried eggs and bacon, beans and sausages. The initiative really took off and soon they were cooking for over thirty guests. The team grew and we realised that some natural multiplication had taken place. This initiative is now 'Manna MSC' – working alongside Haven – reaching the homeless with the love of Jesus.

Chrysalis MSC was another inspired community seeking to reach out to adults with learning difficulties. Again, from very humble beginnings this MSC is establishing a community of love and faith that supports those with disability, their families and carers. Here is an extract from a weekly testimony:

> Chrysalis can only be described as a jigsaw at the moment: slowly but surely the pieces are being fitted in and a bigger picture can be seen. In all honesty, I don't know where we are headed or what God is doing, but I just have such a sense of excitement, God is on the move! At the MSC leaders' weekend away I was very much challenged to lose the 'I can'ts' and realise that our big God can. That is a huge burden-lifter and makes the job a lot easier if I continue to live in this truth! Sunday we looked at God being a God of comfort and everyone has taken a Bible verse home that encourages them at this time. God brought it all together as only He can. There was a real sense of community, support and love and friendships growing. We had a time of prayer which I found especially precious. We are supporting an orphanage out in Zimbabwe which has been on my heart for many years. We have undertaken to pray for those children within the orphanage who have learning disabilities. It was a

precious and touching moment to see members of Chrysalis holding photos of these African children as we prayed together asking for God's hand of blessing on these lives.

There was a wonderful sense of missional entrepreneurialism, what some have called an 'apostolic environment', where our people are continually on the lookout for new opportunities to serve and share their faith. Christmas has become an avalanche of MSC outreach activity. In 2007, as well as themed Christmas services at the centre there were over thirty Christmas outreach activities through the MSC network: Christmas breakfasts, lunches and dinners, carol singing and carol services. The morning services at the centre were overrunning because we were committed to praying for every event. In Chapter 2 I mentioned the King's Chamber Orchestra: classically trained Christian musicians under the anointed baton of Gerard Le Feuvre. Three years later, the same orchestra accepted an invitation to play in a community hall for one of our MSCs. Slap bang in the middle of suburbia these anointed musicians warmed the hearts of a packed community hall with their music and some wonderfully disarming testimony. Seventy per cent of those in attendance were non-churchgoers.

The priesthood of all believers

Exodus 39:32–43 describes how all the Israelites were engaged in assembling the materials that were to be used in building the Lord's tabernacle. Exodus 40:1–33 describes how all the people came together, each contributing their own part, to implement the Lord's plan and assemble the tent. Only when all of the people of

God brought it all together could the plan be accomplished. This was clearly the way that the Lord wanted the job done, and this remains the case.

There is no significant move of God in the whole history of salvation that did not embrace, did not mobilise, the people of God. We are all called. We all have something essential to contribute to the plan. Moses, Luther, Wesley and Seymour all understood that should the Lord choose to give any of us any measure of authority over his people it is primarily that they should be released to make their contribution, to fulfil their calling.

Luther's theses, nailed to the church door and fluttering in the breeze, were the re-commissioning paper for the people of God for the next five hundred years. Wesley set in motion a methodology that would liberate the faithful in proclamation and service. Seymour let loose an entire underclass of men and women to bring in God's Kingdom. And we remain a priesthood of all believers. 'But you are a chosen people, a royal priesthood, a holy nation, a people belonging to God, that you may declare the praises of him who called you out of darkness into his wonderful light' (1 Pet. 2:9).

As we have now exceeded thirty-two 'flavours', we are witnessing the priesthood of all believers released into greater and greater things. As our people are obedient in their call, they are growing to new levels of confidence and their gifting is radiant. In this increase, outreach has become so much more creative and so much bolder. As a centre, I hope that we have become more adept at recognising, releasing and supporting Kingdom entrepreneurs.

A member of St Andrew's Church has his own business. His vision is to make this business a place of work that will support and disciple people who are coming out of addiction. Working with Haven MSC, Manna MSC and with other agencies which are tackling addiction, his desire is to make a place for those who would otherwise struggle to make a fresh start. He is fully aware that this will be a challenging venture. The church centre can support this workplace MSC, providing pastoral cover, discipleship material for those who would like it and weekly prayer for all the Lord is leading them in. I asked him what he was going to call this new MSC. He said that when he had taken on the premises he had noticed that the previous company to occupy the site was called 'Sovereign'. He said, 'I think that's it.'

We also began to see that the MSC structure could give fresh impetus and honour to some long-time ministries within the church. We had resisted the temptation to simply stick labels on pre-existing projects. It was important that we grew some MSCs from scratch so that we could get our operating model up and running. Once that was done, there were existing ministries within the church that were natural candidates for MSC status. For over thirty years St Andrew's had faithfully operated a ministry to mums and those who cared for pre-school children. The ministry was now operating three toddler groups a week, bringing together many people from the wider neighbourhood. I was sure that this outreach was an MSC. It was led by members of the church, it had a clear mission focus and it had a name. I was reluctant to push the MSC agenda upon the leaders but I prayed, 'Lord, would you ask them to ask me if they can be an MSC?' I met with the leadership team one evening, and just as we were finishing the question came: 'Do you mind my asking? Why are we not an MSC?' I was delighted and confessed my prayer. What we have now witnessed is the Lord taking what was a strong ministry to all new heights. The MSC model has raised their profile within the church. Volunteers have increased.

Numbers have increased generally as the MSC operating model has drawn them into the loop of communication, intercession and support. In this context they have really flourished in their outreach. New initiatives have begun – Saturday morning sessions for dads have been really successful. Here was an example of a good thing within the life of the church being made stronger through the MSC strategy.

Our ministry to the elderly was similarly encouraged. For many years the Friendship Club has been operating a midweek day centre where elderly friends from our community are invited to have a hot lunch and to enjoy each other's company. Becoming an MSC brought this ministry to the prayerful attention of the whole church, from where new volunteers have stepped forward to join the existing team. Taking its place alongside all the other MSCs, this wonderfully caring ministry has enabled its members to come to a living faith in Jesus in the autumn of their lives.

Above and beyond our expectations

Back in the desert, when everything was accomplished, when everybody had obediently played their part, the glory of the Lord showed up. Moses wrote, 'Then the cloud covered the Tent of Meeting, and the glory of the Lord filled the tabernacle.' Moses could not even get into the meeting tent. It must have been Moses' intention to go in, otherwise he would not have mentioned this. What the Lord did on this day was clearly more than Moses could ever have imagined or foreseen.

Whatever went through Luther's mind on that cold night in Wittenberg, it is unlikely that with every tap of his hammer he anticipated the global fall from grace of

the Holy Catholic Church and the precipitation of reformation. Could he have remotely anticipated that two
hundred years later a priest serving within a denomination that Luther provoked into existence would hear his
words and have his heart 'strangely warmed'?

Could Wesley have anticipated that in another hundred years or so a young black man would sit in a corri-
dor listening to the teaching of a Spirit-filled minister
raised in Methodism? Did the young William Seymour
have any idea what the Lord was planning as he obediently put down his small, shabby suitcase in downtown
Los Angeles?

There are two very simple principles here. First, when
we have done what the Lord has asked of us, when the
people of God have been mobilised and are working
together to complete the task, you can always rely upon
the Lord to show up. Secondly, his presence, his engagement, will always be vastly disproportionate to anything
that we have brought to the task, more than we could
possibly have imagined.

This has been our experience from day one of this
adventure. The Lord has continually surpassed our
expectations. As I write (January 2008), we are a dispersed-and-gathered church of around 1,600 people.
Seventy-two per cent of our people are in MSCs meeting
on Sundays or midweek (or both). There are also many
people who are passionately working to support the
MSCs but who know that their call is to serve from the
centre. We are not a church with MSCs, we are an MSC
church.

The Lord continually surprises us with new vistas.
Every now and again Judith would receive a call from a
church somewhere in the country asking if we could talk
to them about what we were doing. My inclination has
always been to say yes. We were enormously blessed by

others who were prepared to down tools and help us. Very early on, Shiela Porter, the associate vicar of St George's Deal, got in touch with us. St George's was also on the brink of a major refurbishment project that would mean the loss of their church building for six months or so. Shiela and the vicar of St George's, Chris Spencer, had heard something of what was going on at St Andrew's and were intrigued to hear our story. There were some meetings over lunch and then we were invited to go and speak at St George's. Unfortunately the day before we were due to visit I had just come off a long-haul flight. I am very passionate on this subject, and the lack of sleep and jet lag brought something of a 'hyper' and possibly frenzied quality to my three presentations that day. Mercifully, they were not put off and St George's has since very successfully transitioned to a dispersed-and-gathered model. Talking of St George's experience with MSCs, Shiela shared with me, 'One of our MSCs is working with the severely disabled. Another one has put on the marriage course as part of its mission initiative. Another MSC is resourcing an Alpha course so that the next time they can run it themselves in the local pub.' We keep in touch and greatly appreciate their friendship. It was tremendous to share our 2007 MSC leaders' conference with thirty delegates from St George's. Of this conference, Shiela wrote, 'The Joshua reading [Joshua 1:6–9] finished me off. We set off three years ago into our first MSC with this passage and then it was just a dream. The realisation of what the Lord has done since and is about to do now overwhelmed me. I have returned ready for the next leg.'

At the same MSC leaders' conference we were also joined by thirty delegates from another Anglican church who were poised to make the same transition. There were telephone calls coming in from churches of different denominations across the UK. I was encouraged by this and we went wherever we were invited. In response to the demand we also hosted some day conferences at St Andrew's which were attended by church leaders from all over the country.

Then in late 2006 I took a call from a charming Danish man called Anders Michael. Judith put the call through and told me that he was doing some research on pioneer mission across Europe. It transpired that Anders Michael was carrying out his enquiries on behalf of some American Christian philanthropists whose vision statement is to find burning bushes and to pour gasoline on them! A few weeks later he called me back and told me that we were such a burning bush, and would I and the MSC team like to come to Barcelona and be doused! Anders Michael had searched the length and breadth of Europe and had identified fifteen churches that were pioneering in mission. The plan was to bring these churches together in a learning community called ECPN (European Church Planting Network, www.ecpn.org). From the UK we were to join company with St Thomas' Crookes Parish Church and St Thomas Crookes Philadelphia (Sheffield), Holy Trinity Brompton (London), The Message Trust/ Eden (Manchester and UK) and The Order of Mission (London and Bristol). From Europe there were churches from The Netherlands, Belgium, Sweden, Denmark, Norway and Germany. The St Andrew's team now included Ruth May who, fortunately for us, took up the position of MSC co-ordinator. Ruth immediately saw the big picture and absorbed all the minutiae of detail that made the MSC network function. All of us were hugely encouraged to find kindred spirits from the UK and all over Europe who were pioneering new things and breaking the mould. They asked us if we would like to come back, this time to Budapest, and be doused again.

Budapest was even more explosive. They brought in the American missiologist Neil Cole, who set out some insightful challenges but whose presentation really bothered me. 'If you are just growing out of a single centralised structure,' he said, 'this is not Kingdom multiplication.' What was he talking about? Our whole premise was that the church centre enabled the mission of the priesthood of all believers. Undoubtedly we would come to a point where central resources would be saturated. We had anticipated a day when we would plant a second resourcing centre, but all that seemed a long way off.

That night we were taken out to dinner. On the way to the restaurant I sat right at the back of the bus, feeling a bit depressed. Were we kidding ourselves? By my reckoning of Neil's analysis, we were just playing at church growth. The conference convener, Brent Dolfo, joined me at the back of the bus. As he spoke, I caught the inflection of the Lord's voice: 'This MSC model has the capacity to spread like fire. You need to think locally, nationally and internationally.'

The next day we were encouraged to find some space and to pray. In room 312 of what had once been a hotel for communist leaders I sat and prayed. Brent's words stayed with me and so I paused in my prayers, flipped open the laptop and began to list all the churches in the UK we had shared the MSC strategy with and those that were developing the model. I was amazed to see that I had listed about twelve churches from different denominations across the country. I then felt the Lord's encouragement to list the churches from outside the UK which had approached us with a view to developing the MSC model for themselves. As I typed, the churches just kept coming. Again I also listed about a dozen international churches. I could not believe what I was looking at. Without us even trying, the Lord had brought us into a network of relationships with kindred churches across the UK, Europe and further afield.

Curiously enough, the week before Budapest I had been invited to speak at a church in Norway. They asked if I would go and tell our story and paint pictures for them of what might be. I took my notes and some DVD clips and talked almost continuously for fourteen hours. The Lord had moved powerfully in the life of this Norwegian church. In twenty-eight years under anointed leadership, Jesus had taken them from a small wooden prayer house to state-of-the-art premises that were breathtaking. Among other things, this church had a dance studio, a gymnasium, an indoor football court, a café, a refectory and lecture halls. They even had a room that was a ball-pool for children. You could have landed an aeroplane on their car park, and they had an auditorium for 1,800 people. They were currently six hundred people strong. The Lord had told them that he was going to fill their church but that this would not happen on account of one person's leadership or one pulpit ministry. Neither would he fill the church because of the amazing facilities. This church would be filled when the people of God were mobilised as the priesthood of all believers and led by his Spirit to go out from that place and make their camp among those who do not yet know him. When I described what we were doing and showed them the DVD testimonies they were really moved. Prophetically this Norwegian church has long anticipated an unprecedented move of God. They have faithfully prayed into that conviction for twenty-eight years. Just before I got on the plane to come home, the senior pastor's wife drew me to one side and said, 'In its current form, we know that the church cannot cope with the measure of all that the Lord wants to do. We must mobilise the people of God if we are to faithfully serve God in the revival that is coming.'

Back in Budapest I was reeling at the length of the national and international lists that were now staring back at me from my laptop. I found David, Jenny and Ruth and with a marker pen and a whiteboard drew up these lists for them to see. As I was writing on the board, other ECPN church leaders came towards us, took the marker pen out of my hand and wrote the name of their church on the board. This I had not anticipated. When I returned to the UK and shared all that had happened, Mark was not altogether surprised. When he had first arrived in Chorleywood the Lord had given him a vision of a map with lights coming on all over Europe. There had been a St Andrew's conference, 'Europe Awake!', which had attracted a lot of prayer and interest and yet there was a sense that there was much more to come.

What was now very clear was that we had the potential to multiply on two fronts. Locally we would continue to build MSCs, but at the same time, nationally and internationally we had the opportunity to be a resource to other churches which desired to make the MSC model their own. At our 2007 MSC leaders' conference Mike Breen had been a real inspiration as our speaker. During that weekend he had commented, 'I think the tendency that we have, as Spirit-filled believers, is to get stuck in the "Bless me" culture: "If only I could get blessed one more time." This culture tends to keep the army in the barracks, and of course if the army is in the barracks the enemy has got the rest of the world. That St Andrew's is moving out of the barracks terrifies the enemy and his host, and signals an enormously important moment, a milestone, in English Christianity. What I have seen at St Andrew's is something that is not only important for St Andrew's but a model for other churches.'

Time will tell. Certainly we have watched this model develop from just a handful of pioneers to something larger than we could ever have anticipated. What is clear is that when we faithfully do what the Lord has asked of us and the people of God are mobilised and work together to complete the task, then beyond our comprehension, beyond anything we can imagine, the glory of the Lord will come.

Tracing the rainbow

When I was in my late twenties, before we had children, Elena and I decided to quit the rat race, to leave London and move to the country. I had Devon roots, so we found ourselves a thatched village in the heartland of north Devon where we bought the house of our dreams. All by itself this house said, 'The people who live here have made it!' But actually that was not true. My dad and I would meet up for lunch, and over a pizza he would ask me what it was that I sensed was missing. If I could have told him what it was, that might have been a help. I loved Elena very much but even her love could not fill the gap. There was a quiet sort of despair within me that was only temporarily distracted by the next grand interior decoration scheme or the next big holiday. When we had exhausted all the people we could possibly think of to come and visit us in our big house, it dawned on us that we should probably get to know some people who lived locally and so, as a last resort, we went to the local parish church.

The church was cold and dark and there were more draughts than people. Elena sat down and was immediately told that she was sitting in someone else's pew. The probability of us sitting in someone else's seat was not high but we apologised profusely. There was a curious smell of mildew and wood polish that stayed on your clothes for hours after you had left the building, but there was also a new vicar and his wife Jane, a retired major called Joyce (who had also been a matron), and Rob and Trish. A little bit later Gill and Geoff arrived in the area from Hertfordshire (where they had at one time attended a church that we had never heard of called St Andrew's Chorleywood), and at about the same time we were also invited to lunch by another new couple to the village, Dennis and Sally. Dennis was the new Methodist Superintendent.

There was something about these people that stood out. I was intrigued by and drawn to them all at the same time. They invited us for meals. They were interested in us. One time Trish asked me, referring to my career as a solicitor, 'But how can you do that as a job if you honestly don't find it fulfilling?' and I thought: because it pays the bills on my lovely big house – what a daft question. Just occasionally they would say something like, 'Have you prayed about that?' – which of course we hadn't – and they always spoke about Jesus as if they knew him personally. I decided that I liked them sufficiently not to hold that against them.

The hymn books in the church were so old, they should have been in the British Museum. Deep among the micro-organisms that inhabited these ancient books there was one very old hymn that I developed a soft spot for. It had quite a pretty tune, but there was one line in about the third verse that really caught my attention. 'O joy that seekest me through pain, I cannot close my heart to Thee, I trace the rainbow through the rain, and feel the promise is not vain: that morn shall tearless be.'

I was clueless to explain why, but when I sang this hymn my throat tightened and my eyes filled. Other

hymns from this primordial collection were filled with
words such as 'consubstantial' and exhorted you to raise
the 'Trisagion ever and aye', which was fun to sing but
difficult to apply in the workplace or home. But I knew
what a rainbow was, and the idea of looking out on a
stormy horizon and tracing one with your finger
through the rain was at least a possibility.

A little while later, my friend Richard (the new vicar)
asked us if we would like to be part of an informal group
that was going to meet in a holiday cottage just outside
the village to explore the Christian faith. It turned out
that Jane, Rob, Trish, Joyce, Gill and Geoff were going to
be there as well as Richard, and as they had been so
kind, Elena and I thought that we would encourage the
new vicar and go along. Together with Sally and Dennis
they were beginning to feel a bit like family.

Unbelievably, these meetings in this little holiday cottage had the same effect upon me as the strange rainbow
hymn. I was a bit unsettled by a reference to being born
again as a Christian. In the car on the way home, Rob
said it was not essential to have a big dramatic experience in becoming a Christian but it was necessary to
make a choice; to decide to follow Jesus. The spring
came and the holiday cottage was no longer available, so
Rob said that they were going to start a weekly Bible
study group and I volunteered our house. Elena was
really cross and I had to go out and buy a Bible. They
studied the book of Mark and I helped them along by
asking a lot of questions. I found that I was counting
down the days until the next Bible study group.

One night Rob said, 'There is a speaker coming to a
nearby town to talk about the Holy Spirit and I think
that we should go.' I was a bit suspicious and I said to
Joyce (the retired matron and the major), 'I don't think I
need any of that nonsense.' She said, 'The Lord knows

exactly what you need, so you just get yourself off there and stop complaining.' So I went. I travelled in the back of Richard's car. He was chatting to his assistant and I could not help but overhear their conversation. I recall thinking, 'What a truly horrible job Richard has as a vicar. There is no way you would ever catch me doing a job like that!'

We went to a church in the nearby town of Barnstaple that had once been a railway shed. I was amazed to see that it was packed to the rafters with people of every age. Our friends came with us. Gill and Geoff were seated to our left, Richard and Jane to our right and Rob and Trish right behind us. There was a band with a drum kit and some guitars. They did not sing my rainbow hymn but I liked their music. The speaker got up to address us and to my surprise he spoke just to me. He summarised my life and then he said that I had a realisation that God was moving in my life and that God had plans for me. The talk finished and there was some loud praying. I closed my eyes and began a conversation, 'God, I don't know if you can hear me above all this noise, but Jesus, I am giving you my life. I am saying yes to you without reservation. Whatever you want for my life, I want; whatever, whatever, whatever.' And then I heard singing; glorious singing. I thought thank goodness, the band is back. I opened my eyes to see and there was no band and no choir. I shut my eyes again and the wonderful singing struck up once more.

Shortly afterwards Elena gave her life to Jesus too. So having brought us both to faith, my new family then continued to disciple us. I learned to love the Bible and to hear God's voice through it, because that was what they did. I prayed knowing that God would use my prayers, because that was how they prayed. I introduced my friends and family to Jesus, because that was exactly how they lived. And the aching stopped. Suddenly there was a new love, a new purpose and a sense of God's onward calling. Suddenly my life did not feel such a waste. Dennis thought that he discerned a preacher in me, so he got me some bookings at the local Methodist chapels. On the way home one night from one of these preaching assignments Dennis told me that the Lord had been speaking to him. He told me, 'The Lord wants to build a church without walls.'

Why am I telling you my story? Very simply, if at all possible, I would like to replicate this experience and this revelation of hope, love and purpose in Jesus for every man, woman and child in the United Kingdom and as far overseas as the Lord will allow me. Secondly, my coming to faith was not dependent on some large, super-resourced church. The love of the Father found me in the simple goodness of a community of his people who were prepared to come looking for me. Through their love I discovered that Jesus knew my name, loved me enough to die for my sins and had a plan for my life.

The moment of crisis that the Lord set in my heart that night in Barnstaple was an absolutely necessary part of his plan. It was equally part of his master plan that in a meeting that was about as un-'seeker-friendly' as they come, the family that he had chosen for me came with me and went home with me. Indeed, the very next Monday we met in my sitting room as we always did and they helped me to piece it all together.

The MSC strategy is not just for big churches. It is a way of life that belongs to all the people of God. There are churches of every denomination and size whose people have applied our MSC story in their own context and have seen tremendous fruit. St Andrew's story began with just twelve people who loved the Lord sufficiently to be prepared to go out with that love.

For many of us, the last years at St Andrew's have been about our finding renewed hope in God and in each other. And renewed hope locally has given us bold hope globally. We can fight poverty, we can bring healing to the AIDS pandemic, we can work to bring a stop to people trafficking and we can win this nation and beyond for Jesus Christ. I hear our people sing 'Amazing Grace' with new conviction and restored heart.

Personally, I feel at least forty years older than when this all began and yet I have such a sense that we have only just started. And I have such hope. 'I trace the rainbow through the rain, and feel the promise is not in vain.' By way of completeness, the illness that would shake Elena awake at 2 o'clock in the morning is healed. We are still awake in the small hours of the morning but for very different reasons. We were overwhelmed when the Father blessed us with a beautiful baby daughter, Olivia Rose.

Following my interview for the post of Associate Vicar in 2003, one of the interviewers, Jim Sutton, wrote to Mark and said, 'Like Joshua, I believe that Andrew has seen the Promised Land.' In all humility, I believe that I have, but more importantly, we saw it together. Without the courage and love of his people at St Andrew's I would have nothing to tell.

I was asked to speak at a conference and a church leader approached me with the following question. He said, 'We have had lots of people come and try to sell us the latest model of church growth. A couple of years ago it was cell church and then it was G12 – now we know that they don't work like we were promised. Have you got to the point yet where you realise that what you are selling is not going to work?'

We are truly not in the business of trying to sell anybody anything. We have a story to tell and there are some obvious and ancient principles that we have relearned along the way, but this is not a blueprint. This is not the equivalent of the next fad diet. We tell this story only that you might be inspired to go out and live yours.

The world is watching. The world is not sure whether the Christian church is dead or alive. One moment it is trumpeting our obituary and the next moment it comes back to give the body a poke to see if it can get any response. What I believe we can demonstrate is that the church is very much alive and that rumours of reformation are not unfounded; the Gospel still works and the people of God have still got it in them.

10

NO LIMITS, NO BOUNDARIES

Mark Stibbe

Frank Bartleman was an eyewitness of the great outpouring of the Holy Spirit at Azusa Street in Los Angeles in April 1906 – an outpouring that Drew referred to at the start of the last chapter. Bartleman saw first-hand God moving in extraordinary power, sweeping many people into the Kingdom, healing chronically sick and severely disabled people, setting captives free, breaking down racial divisions and doing countless signs and wonders, many of them recorded for posterity in the *Apostolic Faith* newspaper. In June 1906, several months into a revival whose effects would reach the ends of the earth, Bartleman urged his contemporaries not to miss the moment. As the old saying goes, 'The opportunity of a lifetime must be seized in the lifetime of the opportunity.' Bartleman knew that a great and mighty river of God was moving through Los Angeles and he called out to others to abandon themselves to its currents. As he put it, 'There is a time when the tide is sweeping by our door. We may then plunge in and be carried to glorious blessing, success and victory. To stand shivering on the bank, timid or paralyzed with stupor at such a time, is to miss all, and most miserably fail, both for time and for eternity; oh, our responsibility!'

During the last five years at St Andrew's, we have also seen many come to Christ, being healed and set free, as well as signs and wonders and racial walls tumbling down. It has been a glorious season in which the people of God, moved by the Spirit, have broken out of the four walls of the church building and infiltrated many new, unchurched contexts in Chorleywood and beyond. But all of this could so easily not have happened. It is a sobering thought that none of this might have occurred had I not undergone a profound paradigm shift in my understanding of revival. To put it simply, I could have prevented all this through a lack of spiritual understanding. In this chapter I want to bring some theological reflections to bear upon all that I have seen in recent years. What I am about to share will highlight the importance of not being blind to the new thing God is doing.

Staying current with the current

One of the most critical things in spiritual leadership is to be prophetically in tune with what the Holy Spirit is saying to the church right now. In truth, most of us who are spiritual leaders spend our time in reactive mode, responding to the latest pastoral issues we're confronted with. But it is just as important to be proactive, to look ahead towards God's future and to dream his dreams.

In recent years I have often been asked to speak at prophetic conferences on what the Holy Spirit might be saying and doing right now. In every conference I have made reference to a Bible passage that has for me provided a 'this-is-that' insight into what is going on today. By 'this-is-that' I mean, 'This that the Holy Spirit is doing right now is that which we read about in a particular Bible passage.' The Bible passage in question is Ezekiel 47:1–12.

This text is part of a section of the book of Ezekiel (chapters 40–48) in which a mysterious, supernatural figure takes the prophet Ezekiel on a tour of a brand new Temple. The old Temple, the Temple of Solomon, has recently been destroyed by the Babylonians and all its furnishings removed. The Ark of the Covenant has disappeared for ever, in spite of what Indiana Jones might lead you to believe. The survivors of the violent siege of Jerusalem have been taken into exile in Babylon (modern Iraq) and now they weep over what has happened to the nation of Judah, the city of Jerusalem and the Temple of God. It is in this context, in exile in a foreign and pagan land, that Ezekiel receives an interactive vision of a brand new Temple, far more glorious than the one that Solomon built (one of the wonders of the world). Ezekiel received and communicated the vision contained within chapters 40–48 of his book, and the people were no doubt greatly comforted.

Towards the end of the vision, Ezekiel is given a glimpse of a mighty river of God pouring out of this new Temple. Ezekiel 47:1–12 is a startling picture of the power of the Spirit at work:

> *The man brought me back to the entrance of the temple, and I saw water coming out from under the threshold of the temple toward the east (for the temple faced east). The water was coming down from under the south side of the temple, south of the altar. He then brought me out through the north gate and led me around the outside to the outer gate facing east, and the water was flowing from the south side.*
>
> *As the man went eastward with a measuring line in his hand, he measured off a thousand cubits and then led me through water that was ankle-deep. He measured off another thousand cubits and led me through water that was knee-deep. He measured off another thousand and led me through water*

that was up to the waist. He measured off another thousand, but now it was a river that I could not cross, because the water had risen and was deep enough to swim in – a river that no one could cross. He asked me, 'Son of man, do you see this?'

Then he led me back to the bank of the river. When I arrived there, I saw a great number of trees on each side of the river. He said to me, 'This water flows towards the eastern region and goes down into the Arabah, where it enters the Sea. When it empties into the Sea, the water there becomes fresh. Swarms of living creatures will live wherever the river flows. There will be large numbers of fish, because this water flows there and makes the salt water fresh; so where the river flows everything will live. Fishermen will stand along the shore; from En Gedi to En Eglaim there will be places for spreading nets. The fish will be of many kinds – like the fish of the Great Sea. But the swamps and marshes will not become fresh; they will be left for salt. Fruit trees of all kinds will grow on both banks of the river. Their leaves will not wither, nor will their fruit fail. Every month they will bear, because the water from the sanctuary flows to them. Their fruit will serve for food and their leaves for healing.'

Over the last few years I have fed off the goodness of these words as I have sought to understand a little of what the Holy Spirit has been doing among us as a church at St Andrew's. The critical key for unlocking the significance of this passage is the metaphor of the river. The word 'river' (*nachal* in Hebrew) is used seven times in Ezekiel 47:1–12 and it is a metaphor for the work and the ways of the Holy Spirit. Ever since I first experienced the empowering presence of God's Holy Spirit I have been a 'river' man. Ever since my conversion during a revival at my thoroughly cynical and secular humanistic boarding school, I have loved and longed for the river of God. Indeed, in more jovial moments I have often over the years compared myself to Rat in Kenneth Grahame's classic, *The Wind in the Willows*. Mole says to Rat, 'So this is a River!' 'THE River,' corrected Rat. 'And you really live by the River?' . . . 'By it, and with it, and on it, and in it,' said the Rat. . . . 'It is my world, and I don't want any other. What it hasn't got isn't worth having and what it doesn't know is not worth knowing! Lord! The times we've had together!'

The river is a wonderful metaphor for the Holy Spirit. It is my world too. In fact, it is the world that every true Christian belongs to. It should be the cry of every believer's heart for more of the river of God. Every believer should be like David, who spoke of longing for the presence of God as the deer pants for water at the brook. The river of God is supposed to be our world. We are supposed to live with it, on it and in it all the time. Longing for the river is a noble aspiration. As A.W. Tozer once wrote:

> *I want deliberately to encourage a mighty longing after God. The lack of it has brought us to our present low estate. The stiff and wooden quality about our religious lives is a result of our lack of holy desire. Complacency is a deadly foe of all spiritual growth. Acute desire must be present or there will be no manifestation of Christ to His people. He waits to be wanted.*

Ezekiel 47:1–12 is a great passage of Scripture because it teaches us so much about the river of God, the Holy Spirit. It also warns us about the limitless, uncontainable and mysterious ways of the Holy Spirit. As the prophet reports, 'It was a river that I could not cross, because the water had risen and was deep enough to swim in – a river that no one could cross' (verse 5). There is something gloriously unstoppable and powerful about this river. No one should claim that they have fully comprehended it. A comprehended God is no God at all, as St John Chrysostom once said. Yet at the same time there are lessons to be learned about the ways of the Spirit here. These lessons are highly suggestive for anyone who is trying to discern what the Holy Spirit is doing right now in many churches in the world, including in St Andrew's. Indeed, there is a THIS-IS-THAT dynamic at work here; 'THIS that we see right now in many churches is THAT which we see the river of God doing in Ezekiel 47:1–12.' I will briefly highlight four things about the river in Ezekiel 47 that I believe are helpful for 'staying current with the current'.

1. The direction of the river

It is supremely important to note one simple fact: the river in Ezekiel 47 does not flow *into* God's house; it flows *out of* God's house. The momentum suggests OUTREACH, not INDRAG. Of all the things I am about to reflect on theologically, this is the most significant of all. If you can grasp this one point, and then live out the implications, then you too can experience the paradigm shift necessary to see revival. You too can see the river flow.

Up to the year 2002, it would be safe to say that I operated entirely with an attractional understanding of revival. In other words, I understood revival to be the outpouring of the Holy Spirit upon a church, resulting in masses of people being drawn to God's house in order to hear the Gospel and receive salvation. In many ways, this is the traditional, indeed archetypal, picture of revival. It is the ultimate dream of everyone who lives with a 'come to us' or attractional model of church. It is *Field of Dreams* come true: 'If you build it, they will come.'

There is no doubt that God has moved in this way in previous times. He may again, but probably not in the immediate future in post-Christian Europe. The memory of the Christian story has all but disappeared in Europe. The influence of the Christian church in the UK and Europe is now very insignificant compared to the glory days of the Reformation, when 75 per cent of Europe was converted to a living faith in Christ. Now the figure is more likely to be 7.5 per cent and falling. In such a context, the 'meetings-driven' model of revival is far less likely to occur. Eddie Gibbs makes the point really well. He says in *Church Next*, 'Under the impact of modernism, the church is facing the challenge to re-enter a world that has changed drastically. It cannot hope to regain its previous central position. The church will need to re-enter as a missionary presence with an apostolic stance, living adventurously as a subversive movement, realising afresh its total reliance on the Lord.' That is absolutely right, in my experience. Local churches in Europe must change their whole modus operandi. We are no longer at the centre of every community, able to appeal to a community that is still Christian, and bid them 'come to us'. Rather, we need to 'go to them', planting mission-shaped communities where the unchurched masses of people live, letting these communities grow organically so that they provide what the host communities really need. As Gibbs goes on to say, 'As communities of believers are scattered through every segment of society, non-believers will find those fellowships accessible. . . . In other words, non-believers will be exposed to the Gospel in a highly contextualised form.'

I am a firm believer that the direction of the river of God is not IN towards God's house but rather OUT from the house towards the barren landscape of our secular world. Even some of those who have been most committed to the attractional model are beginning to see

this. Rick Warren's Saddleback Church has been model-
ling attractional evangelism for decades. In many ways
Saddleback has practised it with excellence. Yet in recent
years Rick Warren's laudable involvement with people
with HIV/AIDS has clearly led him to think more about
a 'go to them' as well as a 'come to us' way of being
church. Warren has recently said, 'Jesus modelled, and
the New Testament teaches, both "Come and see" evangelism and "Go and tell" evangelism. Both still work
today, if you understand the mindset and mental barri-
ers of unbelievers.'

Warren is clearly beginning to conduct a conversation
about the merits of an attraction-only model of mega-
church Christianity. That is good, and he is not alone in
that. Warren is right: you can do both 'come to us' *and*
'go to them'. But in the UK and Europe we have to GO
TO THEM first, if they (the lost) are going to COME TO
US. We have to go to their place before they will come to
our place.

In this regard, it is very interesting to see the paradigm shift being exhibited by friends of mine such as
John Arnott. John was at the epicentre of the most
famous western world revival since the Second World
War, the Toronto outpouring in 1994 and subsequently.
John was the senior pastor of the Toronto church visited
by millions in the months and years after the Holy Spirit
fell in January 1994. I was one of those who visited and
whose life was profoundly and irrevocably changed. If
anyone understands a meetings-driven, attractional
model of revival it is John Arnott. And yet in recent
years, now that the midweek renewal meetings are happening less frequently and attracting fewer people,
John's emphasis is changing. I found this statement in an
article John wrote for *Spread the Fire* magazine (out of
Toronto) in 2005: 'If we are going to reach this world for

Jesus, we need a completely new model of "doing church". I don't know why we can't have "church" in homes, offices, schools, coffee shops, or even outside for that matter. Why can't we have church meetings that are facilitated by an army of non-professional yet anointed Christians?'

I have used that quotation a lot over recent years because it has the breath of God all over it. John has clearly seen that the river is pouring out of the church. It may one day pour back in. But we need first of all as God's people to be carried out of the four walls of our buildings into the dry and desert places of our culture, as a dynamic missionary presence. We need to allow the Holy Spirit to reactivate the apostolic imagination in the church. We need above all a 'go to them' ethos at the very core of our individual and collective beings. Nothing less than this will bring about the conversion of the UK and indeed of Europe as a whole. The direction of the river is OUT of the house. As we read in Ezekiel 47:1, 'I saw water coming *out* from under the threshold of the temple.'

2. The increase of the river

As the prophet continues to witness the river of God pouring out of the house, he notices an increase in the river's pace and depth. In verses 3–5 the man accompanying the prophet leads Ezekiel into the river itself. He takes out a measuring rod and begins to gauge the depth of the water. As he does so, the water level starts to rise in stages. First of all it is ankle-deep, then knee-high, then waist-high, then deep enough to swim in. The river does not rise to this final level in one great, sudden deluge. Rather, it rises in degrees, gradually increasing in depth until the point where Ezekiel realises it would be impossible to cross. Now the river is so deep and so fast there is an uncontainable momentum and energy to it. This river is going out from the Temple with ever-increasing depth.

Again, I find this insightful in terms of understanding a different model of revival. To be honest, for many years I held the view that revivals are outpourings of the Holy Spirit that come suddenly. Indeed, if I received a small fee for every talk I have given on God's 'sud-denlys' I would probably be a rich man. I have far too often assumed that God is limited to just one way of moving by his Spirit in a community, a country, even a continent. I have assumed that the only way he moves is dramatically, obviously, suddenly, as on the Day of Pentecost, when according to Acts 2:2, 'Suddenly a sound like the blowing of a violent wind came from heaven and filled the whole house where they were sitting.' I have used this passage many times to justify a 'one-size-fits-all' model of revival. In many ways it has encouraged passivity in God's people. It has led people to sit in the house (like the disciples in Acts 2), waiting for a sovereign, sudden and supernatural outpouring of the Holy Spirit.

I am not alone in having peddled this particular theological model. Not only have I given many talks on God's 'suddenlys', I have heard many too. Indeed, such teaching has been around a long time. Many have been guilty of restricting revival to a sudden invasion of God's Spirit. Here is the nineteenth century's Charles Spurgeon. He said, 'The old stagers in our churches believe that things must grow, gently, by degrees; we must go step by step onward. Concentrated action and continued labour, they say, will ultimately bring success. But the marvel is, all God's works have been sudden.'

Today, I would beg to differ. I don't believe for a moment that God is restricted to one way of awakening his church and reaching out to the lost. In fact, I have sympathy for those whom Spurgeon dismissed as 'the old stagers in our churches'. These old stagers no doubt missed some of the valid points that Spurgeon wanted them to grasp but they got one thing right: God can move gradually too. Of course, this is not as exciting as when God moves suddenly, or so it might at first sight appear. Indeed, there is something less stirring about a message title that reads 'God's graduallys', certainly in contrast to 'God's suddenlys'. It all sounds too much like an excuse for doing things too slowly, and smacks of the old saying, 'Like a mighty tortoise moves the church of God.'

However, speaking about God's 'graduallys' is in no way a licence for gradualism – for dragging our feet and hanging on to old ways when the call is to advance into a new adventure. Speaking about God's 'graduallys' is simply a way of honouring the fact that the Holy Spirit can move in degrees rather than in one sudden manifestation. It honours what we see in Ezekiel 47 – the river of God increasing in depth over time, ankle-deep to knee-deep, knee-deep to waist-high, waist-high to over our heads.

What Ezekiel 47:1–12 offers us is a picture different from the conventional idea of revival. The conventional idea is what I call 'the flash flood model'. Here the Holy Spirit comes suddenly, like a flash flood – a sudden deluge which soaks everything instantly. We have these every so often in Chorleywood. One moment there is no rain, the next there is a monsoon with torrents of water flowing through the town and flooding people's homes. These are dramatic seasons of disorder. They quickly come and they quickly go, leaving everything and everyone startled and lives turned upside down. This is the traditional idea of revival; the flash flood model. From Pentecost to Pensacola, from the first century to the twenty-first century, this is the model we are most accustomed to.

But there is at least one other model, and this I call 'the rising tide model'. In the rising tide model, the water level rises slowly until it reaches the point where we are overwhelmed by grace.

To illustrate this, I often refer to a memorable holiday I had with my children when they were much younger. In their pre-teen days, my four children loved crab-fishing off the quay in Blakeney, north Norfolk. We would rent a house for a week, and the favourite pastime was dropping a line from the side of the quay, baited with bacon, and catching as many crabs as possible. We had many hours of inexpensive fun doing this.

The final time we went, the children were so excited that they sat in the car with their crab lines already baited with bacon. It was a very hot day and a long journey too, and the smell in the car became quite overpoweringly toxic. On arrival at Blakeney three hours or so later, the children piled out of the car and headed straight for the quayside and dropped their lines. Unfortunately, what they hadn't taken into account was the tide. It was out. So there was literally two inches of water into which their lines were cast, and not a sign of a crab. Undeterred, they stayed there hours and hours as the tide began to come in. The water level began to rise and the crabs began to emerge from their hiding places. One by one, crabs were hauled in and placed in buckets of seawater. As the water level rose to the level of the quay itself, scores of other children came out to the seafront, carrying buckets and crab lines too. We, however, had been there about five or six hours by then, so I counted up the number of crabs my children had caught (187 – I remember it well!) and went up and down the harbour asking the other dads how many crabs their children had caught. Making a point is all about timing, so after they had proudly told me their rather pathetic statistics (nothing above twenty), I waited until they asked me how many my children had caught. At this point this very proud father released the current tally – 187 – putting all other competitors to silent shame.

If you want my take on what has happened at St Andrew's over the last five years, I would say we have been witnessing a 'rising tide' model of revival. Week by week, month by month, year by year, the water level has been rising. We have been out fishing in all of our mission-shaped communities. This is, after all, a move of God that encourages fishing. As Ezekiel heard, 'There will be large numbers of fish, because this water flows there and makes the salt water fresh; so where the river flows everything will live. Fishermen will stand along the shore; from En Gedi to En Eglaim there will be places for spreading nets. The fish will be of many kinds – like the fish of the Great Sea.'

Throughout our MSCs we have been fishing when the water level has been low and we have been fishing when the water level has been rising. Reading Drew's chapter on the presence of God (Chapter 7), I am left in no doubt that the water level is higher than it was five years ago. Even if it is still only knee-high, I am still immensely encouraged. God's children have been out fishing for men, as Peter was commanded to do in Luke 5:10. Unchurched people are being caught by the Gospel message. Mike Breen said in 2006, 'If you listen to the testimonies, it is clear that the river is here. In other words, you are already in revival mode.' God has been moving gradually by his Spirit. The water level of the river is increasing. The number of those being saved is rising daily. This is revival, but not as we've known it. It is one of 'God's graduallys'. If this means that it will stay longer and have a more lasting impact, then – in the immortal words of Captain Jean-Luc Picard – 'Make it so!'

3. The impact of the river

In chapter 1 I quoted Meic Pearse's important paper delivered at King's College, London in 2002 entitled 'Revivals as Historically Situated Events'. Meic gave this paper as a seminar in a conference dedicated to revival, where I also was asked to give a lecture. Meic's paper was powerfully used by God to transform my understanding of revival. In the course of his presentation, Meic made this bold comment: 'Contemporary Britain and other woefully under-evangelised societies can indeed experience revival. . . . But it will not look like the Day of Pentecost, or like Jonathan Edwards' meeting room.' He spoke about another model of revival, a much more gradual model in which it is impossible to identify or prophesy a start-date. He warned against reading the Bible simply as a book, 'as if it has only one model to offer us'. And he spoke eloquently about being realistic about our historical context in the UK and in Europe, which demands a more gradual and hardworking approach, even if this is unpopular with both the slothful 'ordinary Christian' and the 'would-be pulpit superstar'.

From what I have written already you can see my indebtedness to Meic Pearse's lone voice in the wilderness of current revival theology. In recent years I have come to see the truthfulness of Meic's perspective from my own experience as a leader of a church in what I might call 'alternative revival mode'. The amazing things we have seen did not involve us holding nightly meetings with a 'come to us' approach. Rather, what was involved was a slow and prayerful process – often with sweat and tears – in which the whole of our church was mobilised to go out and establish mission-shaped communities where there was little or no Gospel witness. What we have seen did not come suddenly, like a mighty deluge of hard rain. Rather, it has happened gradually, increasing from ankle-deep to knee-high, like the river of God in Ezekiel 47. As one of our staff, Dr John Cowan, said to us recently, if the river is knee-high, all you have to do is get really low before the Lord and you'll already be in over your head.

Ezekiel saw something about the ways of the Holy Spirit that I believe with all my heart is tremendously important for our times. THIS indeed is THAT. He saw something critical about the direction and the increase of the river of God flowing from the future Temple. And he also saw something extremely significant about its impact in verses 7–9:

> *When I arrived there, I saw a great number of trees on each side of the river. He said to me, 'This water flows toward the eastern region and goes down into the Arabah, where it enters the Sea. When it empties into the Sea, the water there becomes fresh. Swarms of living creatures will live wherever the river flows.'*

To this we should add verse 12:

> *Fruit trees of all kinds will grow on both banks of the river. Their leaves will not wither, nor will their fruit fail. Every month they will bear, because the water from the sanctuary flows to them.*

What Ezekiel sees is the impact of the river on the ecology of the landscape. He sees the life-giving impact of the Holy Spirit both in marine life and indeed in agriculture and horticulture. Even the great Arabah, the place whose name means 'depression', is affected by the animating properties of this supernatural river that flows from the sanctuary. Wherever the river goes, it leaves 'abundance' in its wake – an abundance of fish and an abundance of fruit. This is a river whose impact is environmental.

And therein lies another major difference between the old and the new paradigms of revival. In the old paradigm, what really mattered was that individuals were saved. As God poured out his Holy Spirit in Northampton, USA in the 1730s, what mattered to Jonathan Edwards were the 'Narratives of Surprising Conversions'. Edwards delighted in the impact of the Holy Spirit on the lives of individuals who had formerly been spiritually dead but now, thanks to the life-giving work of the Spirit, had come alive in Christ. These were the testimonies that Edwards wanted to tell – individual sinners in the hands of an angry God, whose lives had been saved by believing in the finished work of the Cross.

What is remarkable about the river of God in Ezekiel 47 is the way its impact moves beyond the individual to the ecological. The fish are affected, and so are the trees. Now I am not suggesting for one moment that the new paradigm of revival will not focus on the salvation of individuals. It will. In the new model of revival, there will still be a great emphasis on sharing the Gospel and leading people to saving faith in Christ. I am as committed to this as I was over thirty years ago when I entered an eternal friendship with Jesus Christ on the streets of Winchester during a wonderful move of the Holy Spirit.

The glorious message of the Cross is what saved me then and it is still what saves people today. It has not lost its ancient power. Just in the last few weeks I have seen and heard of people who have made a first-time commitment to Christ through hearing the Gospel message in our mission-shaped communities, as well as at the church centre. The salvation of individual souls through dynamic Gospel ministry will always be central here.

At the same time, the old paradigm of revival can lead to an overemphasis on individuals. While I am convinced that we are supposed to invest in saving souls, I am also convinced that the Father's dream is bigger than that. The Father's dream is for the planet as well as people. Preaching throughout the summer of 2007 on Romans chapter 8, I was reminded of the cosmic nature of the Father's saving plan. The death and resurrection of Jesus Christ not only bring spiritual orphans into their justification and adoption, but also bring the whole of creation nearer to its liberation. The whole of creation is, after all, groaning in travail for God's glory, waiting for the manifestation of the adopted sons and daughters of God. As I declared this truth in a sermon at St Andrew's in July 2007, Drew Williams ran out of the church! A cloud had formed over the building and nowhere else in Chorleywood. A shaft of light was beaming down into the sanctuary. A perfect rainbow had formed as I was speaking about the current work of the Spirit being for our environment, not just for ourselves. It was like a divine YES to the message.

When I was speaking in an orphanage in Uganda in March 2007 I was not only moved by the way the leaders had brought orphans into a saving relationship with Jesus, but I was also impressed by the way in which even the natural surroundings seemed to be affected too. The avocados were the biggest I had ever seen.

Everywhere, nature seemed to be responding too. As the sons and daughters of God were being made manifest to this particular environment, it was as if the land had been healed.

This idea of the 'healing of the land' has become increasingly important to me in recent years. In 2 Chronicles 7:13–14 we read:

> *'When I shut up the heavens so that there is no rain, or com-*
> *mand locusts to devour the land or send a plague among my*
> *people, if my people, who are called by my name, will humble*
> *themselves and pray and seek my face and turn from their*
> *wicked ways, then will I hear from heaven and will forgive*
> *their sin and will heal their land.'* ·

In this famous revival text King Solomon is told by the Lord what to do when he and his kingdom are confronted by ecological disaster – when there is drought, famine and plague. Four things are mentioned by way of an antidote: humbling ourselves, praying, seeking God's face and turning from wickedness. These are followed by three promises: 'If you do these four things, I will (1) hear from heaven, (2) forgive your sin and (3) heal the land.'

In truth, the emphasis in revival history has almost exclusively been on the second of these three promises, on the forgiveness of sins. The focus has been on getting individuals to repent of their sins and receive forgiveness at the Cross. None of this should be undermined or neglected in the future. At the same time, the promise includes the healing of the land as well, and land means land. It is to be taken literally and not metaphorically.

Here again we see something of the difference between the old and the new paradigms of revival:

Old Paradigm

• Individual

New Paradigm

• Environmental

In the old paradigm, the focus is on the transformation of individuals. In the new paradigm the emphasis will be on that and much more – on the transformation of society, of the environment, of the planet. Even some of the chief proponents of the old model of revival have caught glimpses of this bigger picture. Not long ago I found this remarkable quotation from the writings of John Wesley: 'I believe in my heart that faith in Jesus Christ can and will lead us beyond an exclusive concern for the well-being of other human beings to the broader concern for the well-being of the birds in our backyards, the fish in our rivers, and every living creature on the face of the earth.' These words have been important to us at St Andrew's. We want to see whole communities transformed (including whole environments) as well as individuals.

4. The fruit of the river

There is one final observation to make about the river of God in Ezekiel 47:1–12, and here again we will discover some key insights into the new paradigm of revival. The final sentence of the passage refers to the trees that grow and flourish on the banks of the river. The prophet observes that 'their leaves will not wither, nor will their fruit fail. Every month they will bear, because the water from the sanctuary flows to them. Their fruit will serve for food and their leaves for healing.'

Notice here how the fruit from the trees serves for feeding the hungry and healing the sick. Here we see the integration of two aspects of the church's mission that are far too frequently divorced: these are the social justice and the supernatural aspects. The idea of feeding strongly suggests the importance of bringing practical help to the poor. The idea of healing equally strongly suggests bringing divine health to the sick. In my experience, these two agendas are usually separated. Some churches emphasise social justice but neglect altogether supernatural healing. Other churches emphasise supernatural healing but totally neglect social justice. The fruit from the river of God in Ezekiel 47:12 is not so easily divided. It is BOTH-AND, not EITHER-OR. It is both mercy AND miracles.

I took a team from St Andrew's to Uganda in March 2007. Our agenda was to bring the Father's love to the fatherless, particularly the many orphans that Uganda has today (10 per cent, approximately, of its population, and 50 per cent of its children). In one orphanage we were taken to the 'Baby House', where a number of babies were being looked after by an amazing American missionary called Robyn and her Ugandan team. We were told that many of these babies were HIV-positive.

The Holy Spirit had been challenging me about developing an integrated spirituality of mercy and miracles, so we took each of these babies in our arms and appealed first of all to God's justice, declaring that it was unfair that these children did not have a hope for a future. We proclaimed Jeremiah 29:11 over each of them and appealed to the Father's justice and mercy, in Jesus' name. We then appealed to God's mighty power. We asked him in Jesus' name to stretch out his hand in signs and wonders and to perform miracles in the lives of each one. As we held these babies, the four of us – all men – were moved to tears as we pleaded with the Lord of Heaven.

In December 2007 I took a team back to the same orphanage and we went once again to the Baby House. Robyn was full of joy. The blood tests had come back from the hospital and every single one of these children was HIV-negative – they were AIDS-free. As Robyn said, this is a definite miracle. We all praised God and prayed once again for each of the babies, that they would all grow up to live lives that made a difference for Jesus in the country of Uganda.

I have become absolutely and unshakeably convinced that the greater the mercy, the greater the miracles will be. Our God is not a God who tears things apart. He is a God who brings things together. As a friend of mine is fond of saying, 'The devil isolates, but Jesus integrates.' That is so true. As the river of God is moving in our church today we can see that the Lord is bringing back together what human beings have put asunder. The most obvious of all of these divine remarriages is the reintegration of the Word and the Spirit, the Bible and the power of God. But there are other aspects of the church's life which the Holy Spirit is busily bringing back together. Mercy and miracles are very much on the list. The Father wants our mission to be a holistic mission – a mission in which words, works and wonders are not separated but integrated.

This, then, marks a final point of departure from the old model of revival. Very often previous revivals have tended to emphasise the Word only. They are characterised by a great hunger for the Word of God and a great revival of Gospel preaching.

A few revivals have had a noble emphasis on works – on good works flowing out of saved lives. I write this on the final day of 2007, the year of the two-hundredth anniversary of the abolition of the slave trade, thanks principally to the tireless efforts of William Wilberforce. A few revivals or awakenings have had a massive impact on issues of social justice.

Very few revivals have seen a resurgence of wonders – of gifts of the Spirit, notably healing, prophecy, speaking in tongues, miracles and so forth. Very often these manifestations of the Spirit's power have been either neglected or even despised as a result of wrong theology.

In the new model of revival this fragmentation of originally integrated emphases will no longer be witnessed. Those committed to the river of God as described in Ezekiel 47 will not split apart what God has joined together. Rather, as in the mission statement of Jesus in Luke 4:18–19, there will be a restored emphasis on preaching good news to the poor (the Word), releasing the oppressed (works) and bringing recovery of sight to the blind (wonders). These things will not be separated but harmonised as at Azusa Street in 1906, where words, works and wonders were brought together in the birthplace of the now worldwide Pentecostal movement.

Only two things will prevent Christians from entering into such an Ezekiel 47 move of God. The first is spiritual myopia. It is fascinating to my mind that the man accompanying Ezekiel asks him in verse 6, 'Son of man, do you see this?' The man in the vision is asking the prophet whether he can see the river of God and what it is doing. You would think that a river that spectacular would be hard to miss! But there is a point to the question. Some people can be right in the midst of a great work of the Holy Spirit and not have the eyes to see what God is doing. At St Andrew's over the last five years there have been a few people who simply have not been able to see (or maybe not wanted to see) the extraordinary goodness of what the Holy Spirit is doing. It is as if there was something wrong with their spiritual eyesight, so that they were unable to perceive prophetically what was happening right in front of them. As I have observed this with sadness, I have come to understand more and more why the mystery man of Ezekiel 40–48 asks the prophet whether or not he sees things. People either see it or they don't.

If the first obstacle is myopia the second is nostalgia. There is a curious verse in Ezekiel 47:1–12 where we read, 'But the swamps and marshes will not become fresh; they will be left for salt' (verse 11). The river brings life and refreshment everywhere it goes, except for the swamps and the marshes. Here more than anywhere in the passage I am aware of the dangers of *eisegesis* – of reading into the text what was never intended. But it seems to me that one thing we can say is that the swamps and marshes are the places where old water collects, mixed with silt and mud. For me this represents the places where people can't let go of the previous revival. In my experience, sometimes the greatest enemies of a new move of the Holy Spirit are the champions of the last great move. I know this has been said by many before me, but my story is not that opposition has come from Anglican traditionalists but rather from a tiny number of people who have been involved in a previous move of the Spirit. I believe David Watson was making the same point when he once made this very challenging remark:

> Christian work is constantly crippled by clinging to blessings and traditions of the past. God is not the God of yesterday. He is the God of today. Heaven forbid that

we should go on playing religious games in one corner
when the cloud and fire of God's presence have moved
to another.

The greatest obstacles to the new paradigm of revival
are myopia and nostalgia. We have needed to be vigilant
in both areas.

Back to Azusa Street

Over the weekend of 7–9 April 2006, St Andrew's witnessed scenes I doubt have ever been seen in its nearly
100-year history. To celebrate the exact centenary of the
outpouring of the Spirit at Azusa Street in April 1906, I
invited my dear friend Bishop Joseph Garlington, his
wife Barbara and his entire choir to come and lead us in
our church weekend. Bishop Joseph is the senior leader
of the Covenant Church in Pittsburgh. He is an African-
American with a stunning singing voice and a unique
preaching style. His wife Barbara has a very effective
healing ministry. The Covenant Church choir is one of
the most exciting groups of singers I have ever heard.
Racially integrated, they bring joy to a worship event
which in my experience is absolutely unique. That
weekend, the roof nearly came off as God's people
crammed into St Andrew's and sang to the Lord.

There were many great results from the weekend, not
least the washing away of the colour line in the blood of
Christ, as at the first outpouring at Azusa Street in 1906.
As a result of that visit, we now have a much more
racially mixed congregation. This has brought terrific
gladness to my heart since one of the major emphases of
my life in recent years has been racial reconciliation, and
particularly a breaking down of dividing walls between

black and white churches in the UK and the USA.

The most powerful effect of all, however, was a quantum leap in our level of faith in what God can do. My own denomination, the Anglican Church, can be somewhat suspicious of people with strong faith. We tend to go for SURVIVAL where our Pentecostal brothers and sisters go for REVIVAL. I am not saying that my Pentecostal friends are theologically flawless (who is?). Nor am I saying that I myself feel called to make St Andrew's a Pentecostal church. What I am saying is that many of my friends in this particular world really believe that all things are possible. They simply believe that we are not called to manage decline but rather to oversee the expansion of the Kingdom of God through the local church. I like hanging out with such people, simply because they give me a much-needed faith-lift.

While the Garlingtons were with us, they and their choir taught us a new song that stirred the hearts of many. It was a song with a very simple tune first composed in Zimbabwe, but it contained the words 'No limits, no boundaries, I see increase all around me.' At that time the MSC adventure had been underway for nearly three years and we had already seen considerable growth. But as we all sang that song during the weekend, something broke in our lives and I believe it was that SURVIVAL mentality which stems so much from the very negative thinking that many (especially Anglicans) are used to hearing. Suddenly, a large army of believers rose up, as at Azusa Street, with the belief that all things are possible and that we hadn't seen anything yet. Since that time we have grown through innovative mission to a church of 1,600 men, women and children, with no sign of anything less than constant growth in the future.

As our friends left to return for Pittsburgh, many of us – through tear-filled eyes – saw a different horizon from the one that we had seen before. We saw in our spirits the possibility of a massive and spontaneous expansion of the church – a breaking out of God's people into even greater apostolic exploits. We saw mission-shaped churches developing not just in the region of Chorleywood but all over the country and indeed the continent and beyond. Some of us had previous dreams resurrected – in my case, the dream of a Europe awake in the Holy Spirit. We saw mission-shaped communities breaking out of apostolic bases all over the UK and continental Europe. We saw lights breaking out in the darkness, joined together by golden gossamer lines representing new Kingdom networks. We saw revival from a brand new perspective. More than that, we saw the stirrings of a new Reformation – God's people set free to be an army of the Father's love, taking new ground with an entrepreneurial spirit the like of which has rarely if ever been seen before. We saw such things and we knew that the future of the west and maybe even the world depends upon it.

CONCLUSION

Mark Stibbe

In the first few weeks of 2008 I was speaking at a leaders' conference and a young man stood up during a time of quiet. With some trepidation he delivered a prophetic word to the whole of the movement he represented. He told the church leaders present to stop behaving like Pharaoh. He said that for too long, leaders have been trying to build their own empires, whipping their people like slave-drivers, attempting to build a huge monument to their own ministries. He told them in quiet but compelling words that God would not stand for this any longer and that he wanted leaders like Moses, not like Pharaoh. In other words, he wanted leaders to be liberators, not slave-drivers. His word over every leader present was, 'Let my people go, that they may worship me in the desert.'

As I listened to this, everything in my heart was shouting 'Amen!' In many ways, this prophetic message was a perfect summary of my ministry at St Andrew's. During the first phase of my time at St Andrew's I was sometimes guilty of a Pharaoh style of leadership. I don't think it is unfair to say that I was trying to build a huge mega-church – a place where a big crowd would come around my pulpit ministry. I had even made the first steps towards acquiring the land to build a massive and unbelievably expensive resource centre. I could feel the drive within my heart to do this, and I am fairly sure that many others around me felt driven as a result. Driven leaders, after all, end up driving other people.

But then, after we left the building and formed into MSCs at the start of 2005, I distinctly remember waking up and hearing my Heavenly Father say, 'Let my people go, that they may worship me in the desert.' I recall the feeling of conviction I had on hearing these words, realising that I had been like Pharaoh when everything within me wanted to be like Moses. Today, with nearly three-quarters of our church in MSCs worshipping God in the desert of our post-Christian landscape, I can sleep a little more easily. It has been an amazing and sometimes extremely costly journey, but I really believe that we have liberated people from building pyramids and released them into the Promised Land of a new reformation.

Does this mean I have no regrets? Not at all! There are a number of areas where I wish things had been very different. Let me identify just four.

First of all, launching out into MSCs was a huge risk. I remember having a chat with Mike Breen and asking him, 'Mike, what is the biggest threat to the goodness of what I am overseeing here?' Without hesitation he answered, 'Maverick leaders – leaders who want to pursue their own agenda rather than the Lord's.' That certainly hit home. Our MSC leaders have been incredibly loyal to the vision and have done an astonishing work on the frontiers of mission, reaching out to the unchurched in creative and daring ways. They have been extremely faithful and Drew and I have nothing but praise for them. But like Moses, we have also run into situations of conflict, where differences of vision and strategy have opened up. Fortunately these have been extremely infrequent but it has not always been a smooth sea.

The second area where I have regrets concerns my relationship with local Anglican clergy. If the truth be told, I could have invested more in my relationships with the vicars in whose parishes we established MSCs. When it became clear that we were going to be without our building from January to September 2005, I wrote a letter to every single vicar about what we were doing. At that time I honestly thought it was a temporary nine-month stop-gap solution, and I said so. I only recall having two positive replies to these letters. These both very graciously extended the hand of friendship, welcoming our people into their parishes in a spirit of generosity and partnership. For the rest, there was silence. This silence continued until after our building was returned to us and many of our MSCs decided to stay out in the communities they had started to serve so well. At that stage I began to pick up some flak, understandably. In retrospect it would have been better if I had cleared my diary and invested in a period of discussion and clearer explanation with local clergy. That I did not do so is a continuing source of regret.

The third area where I have regrets concerns our relationship with the diocese. When I was appointed Vicar of St Andrew's it was my deep desire that the church's relationship with its diocesan bishop would be similar to the one Holy Trinity Brompton (HTB) has had with the Bishop of London. In the case of HTB, the Bishop of London has had such a strong vision and longing for mission that he has allowed the leaders of this larger church to plant missionary congregations beyond the borders of their own parish. It was precisely this kind of 'out of the box' thinking that I and St Andrew's wanted with our own diocese. We could have done more to have facilitated such a creative partnership. My hope is that in the future this will be possible.

The fourth and final area of grief has been to do with those who have felt that the transition into an MSC church has been an unwelcome reality. There were some who really liked the attractional model of church and who really missed it when we morphed into a gathered-and-dispersed congregation. A few of these have been disempowered and even alienated by the move to a lifeboat-station model of church. Looking back, I was not as sensitive as I might have been when this happened. Even though many hundreds were released in their gifts and ministries, there were a few for whom the transition meant their particular skills (more fitted to a gathered model of church) were no longer going to be as necessary. I am sure I would handle that situation differently if I had my time again.

So I do have some regrets and I have made some mistakes. But if you pushed me to the wall and said, 'Would you lead the church in the same direction all over again?' my answer would be a definite 'Yes'. In the last few weeks we have had by far the biggest Alpha course ever, as MSC members have hosted tables and have brought new friends with them from the communities that they are serving. This month the MSC network has embarked on 106 different outreach projects (that is nearly three per day) and nearly sixty people have given their lives to Jesus Christ. Tomorrow eight teenagers are being baptised. In addition, we have a greater amount of outreach to the poor than we have ever had. And equally encouraging, as the sound of revival is in the air, we have seen an increase in miracles. Indeed, while we have experienced the Breakout, now it seems we are experiencing the Outbreak!

There is therefore much more to celebrate than to lament in the story of St Andrew's over recent years. You will always find a few in every church who will moan, criticise, gossip and even slander. But they are the minority and every congregation has them. But for the most part, the unsung heroes of St Andrew's church have risen to a great challenge and done mighty exploits for the Lord in mission. They have done so willingly and cheerfully, without complaining about the cost to them in time, energy and finance. They have heard the call to launch the lifeboats and they have given their all to reaching those in peril on the sea of life. I am immensely proud of them and give thanks to my Father for them in prayer.

Now my time is drawing to an end as Vicar of St Andrew's Church Chorleywood. I have discerned and responded to a call to focus on the main passion of my life, which is to address the global pandemic of fatherlessness and to take the Father's love to the fatherless. This involves me finishing as Vicar of St Andrew's and taking a massive step of faith. All I can say is that only a genuine call of God would lead me to leave a church like this and a community like Chorleywood. But then the whole of the last twelve years has been an exercise in the art of letting go.

Now St Andrew's, as it enters its hundredth year, awaits a new vicar and a new season. Moses is about to leave the scene and it is time for a new leader to take the vibrant and fruitful mission of this church to the next level. This book is about to end, and so is a chapter in the life of this extraordinary church. But the great MSC adventure is poised to continue and I am excited about what the Father intends to do as this mission-shaped church expands throughout the UK, into Europe and beyond.

BIBLIOGRAPHY

Barna, G., *Revolution* (Tyndale House Publishers, 2005).

Bonnke, R., *Lost at Sea* DVD introduction to the Full Flame series (Christ for All Nations, 2007).

Collins, J., *Good to Great* (Random House, 2001).

Collins, J. and J. Porras, *Built to Last* (HarperBusiness, 1997).

De Pree, M., *Leadership Jazz* (Doubleday, 1992).

Frost, M. and A. Hirsch, *The Shaping of Things to Come* (Hendrickson Publishers, 2003).

Gibbs, E. and I. Coffey, *Church Next* (Inter-Varsity Press, 2001).

Hentoff, N., *Boston Boy* (Paul Dry Books, 2001).

Hosier, J. and L. Hoeksma, *Entertaining Angels* (Kingsway Publications, 2007).

McManus, E., *An Unstoppable Force* (Group Publishing, 2001).

McManus, E., *Soul Cravings* (Thomas Nelson Publishers, 2007).

Michelli, J., *The Starbucks Experience* (McGraw-Hill Professional, 2006).

Ogden, G., *The New Reformation* (Zondervan, 1990).

Ravenhill, L., *Heart Breathings* (Harvey Christian Publishers, 1995).

Schultz, H., *Pour Your Heart Into It* (Hyperion, 1998).

Stibbe, M., *Fire and Blood* (Monarch Books, 2001).

Stibbe, M., *Times of Refreshing* (Zondervan, 1995).

Stibbe, M., *The User's Guide to Christian Belief* (Lion Hudson, 2007).

Tozer, A.W. *The Pursuit of God* (Authentic, 2004).

Warren, R., *The Purpose Driven Life* (Zondervan Publishing House, 2003).

Wheatley, M., *Leadership and the New Science* (Berret-Koehler, 2006).

For Details of Mark Stibbe's Other Resources

Contact: The Father's House Trust
www.fathershousetrust.com

One Touch from the King . . . Changes Everything

Mark Stibbe

Mark Stibbe writes:

'My message in this book is this: just one divine touch
. . . that's all it takes. God can radically transform your
situation with just one royal touch. A moment of divine
contact can bring an invasion of heaven into your world.
I believe with all my heart that Jesus can touch our lives
today. When that happens, we see miracles.

'Healings can happen gradually; miracles happen
instantly. Healings can involve a process; miracles
involve a crisis. Healings can be partial; miracles are
total. Healings can involve remissions; miracles involve
cures.

'When I talk about "one touch from the King" I am referring to the gift of miracles – an instant, total, critical
transformation.

Don't you long for that kind of manifestation today?'

978-1-86024-597-8

The
Resurrection
Code

Mary Magdalene
and the Easter
Enigma

Mark Stibbe

The Resurrection Code offers fresh and original insights into one of the oldest and most cherished stories – the story of the encounter between Mary Magdalene and the risen Jesus, as told in John's Gospel.

Mark Stibbe's insightful analysis provides solutions to various puzzles in the 'Easter enigma' recorded in John chapter 20, such as:

- the identity of the beloved disciple, present at the empty tomb
- the probable timing of Jesus' resurrection (which differs from the usual Sunday sunrise scenario)
- the reason why John includes very precise details about the nature and the placing of Jesus' grave clothes in the tomb
- the way in which the two angels, positioned at both ends of the slab where Jesus' body had been lying, offer the interpretative key that unlocks the deeper meaning of these momentous events
- why Jesus says, 'Do not touch me!' to Mary Magdalene, and a few verses later invites Thomas to touch his hands and side

Reading *The Resurrection Code* is a stimulating experience. The adventure of finding 'secrets' that John has embedded in his gospel will appeal to everyone with an inquisitive mind.

978-1-86024-491-9

Prophetic Evangelism

When God Speaks to those who Don't Know Him

Mark Stibbe

In this compelling book, Mark Stibbe argues that God wants to speak prophetically into the lives of unbelievers, waking them up to the fact that Jesus is alive and he knows their every thought, word and action.

There are many biblical examples of God's people using prophecy in their witness to unbelievers. Jesus used prophecy in his ministry to seekers. After Pentecost, God gave the gift of prophecy to believers as one resource among many in their witness to the world. Furthermore, Christians today receive prophecies for those who don't know Christ, often with immediate and life-changing effects. This book contains many such testimonies.

This is the first book to explore how the gift of prophecy can be used with potent effects in our outreach to non-Christians.

978-1-86024-457-5